Southern Cakes

Southern Cakes

Sweet and Irresistible Recipes for Everyday Celebrations

by NANCIE McDERMOTT
photographs by BECKY LUIGART-STAYNER

CHRONICLE BOOKS
SAN FRANCISCO

Library of Congress Cataloging-in-Publication Data available.

ISBN 978-0-8118-5370-5

Manufactured in CHINA.

Designed by ALICE CHAU.

Food styling by JAN MOON and ANA KELLY.
Prop styling by FONDA SHAIA.
Photo assistance by BOO GILDER.

10 9 8 7 6 5 4

CHRONICLE BOOKS LLC
680 Second Street
San Francisco, California 94107
www.chroniclebooks.com

For their excellent, insightful, and creative work on behalf of this book, I am grateful beyond measure to Bill LeBlond, my editor, and Amy Treadwell of Chronicle Books.

For their extraordinary and thoughtful efforts on my behalf, I am thankful to Lisa Ekus, my literary agent, and Jane Falla of Lisa Ekus Public Relations.

For their generosity in sharing recipes, baking knowledge, and wisdom, I offer my deepest gratitude to Cornelia Walker Bailey, Jackie Bays, Waddad Habeeb Buttross, Edna Faust, Marcie Cohen Ferris, Carmen Flowers, Trish Good, Libbie Hall, Edna Hall Gambling, Frances Fleming Hunter, Virginia Dockery McDermott, Verna Suitt McDermott, James McNair, Robert Mullis, Lily Nichols, Suzanne O'Hara, Sybil Pressly, Marilyn Meacham Price, George Pyne, Milo Pyne, Sallie Ann Robinson, Amy Rogers, Ann Romines, Kathy Starr, John C. Whitener, Helen Hudson Whiting, and Blanche Williams.

For their energy, enthusiasm, and humor, I thank my wonderful and cherished friends, Harvey Bolgla, Phillis Carey, Deb Gooch, Karen Johnson, Rob Lehmann, Dean Nichols, Jill O'Connor, and Bob and Vada Satterfield.

For their love, patience, wisdom, and encouragement, I thank my parents; my sisters, Linda Lloyd McDermott and Susanne McDermott Settle; and my wonderful family, Will, Camellia, and Isabelle Lee.

To my wonderful daughters,
CAMELLIA DAO-LING McDERMOTT LEE and
ISABELLE DAO-AHN McDERMOTT LEE,
who make my life a piece of cake:

delicious, rich, and sweet.

Table of CONTENTS

INTRODUCTION

Writing this book has been an extraordinary journey. Born and raised in the Piedmont region of North Carolina, I grew up nurtured, body and soul, by wonderful Southern home cooking. I come from a family of home cooks, for whom baking was neither a remarkable skill nor a hobby, but rather, a task of home life. It was messier than laundry, more creative than ironing, less fun than gardening for my mother, and satisfying to all of us, being a family captivated by food.

My mother was raised on a dairy farm by a mother who cooked a hot breakfast well before dawn every day of the year, fed the entire farm crew a huge, hearty lunch at noon, and regularly put on a fine Sunday dinner for a dozen people. And my grandmother didn't miss church or serve anything cold except milk.

My mother had a gifted teacher in my grandmother, right there in the kitchen. But by the time she was cooking for a family in a kitchen of her own, the world had spun, as it always does, to a new configuration. Instead of cooking for a crew of family members and employees, she was putting three square meals together for a fifties-era family. Unlike her mother, who learned to cook the food she had grown up eating from the women in her family, my mother paid attention to books and magazines full of recipes and kitchen wisdom.

I felt quite at home in my grandparents' farmhouse, just as I did in my family's brick house with carport, breakfast nook, swing set, and pine-paneled den. In my everyday life, I enjoyed the television set, coloring books, peanut butter sandwiches, and meatloaf at home, just as I loved the fishing pond, rope swing, hayloft, and chicken coop on my grandparents' farm. Since we lived only 30 miles away, my sisters and I lingered and lounged around the farm on weekends and during the summer, never far from the kitchen and ever eager to see what good things the huge kitchen table might hold at the next meal. Watching, and eventually helping, my grandmother bake was one of my greatest treats.

She made biscuits in a shallow wooden dough tray, transforming flour, lard, and buttermilk into perfect little pillows of hot bread, exquisite with butter and divine with honey or preserves from the pantry. She mixed cakes in a deep, wide, lightweight, red-rimmed white-enamel bowl, which doubled as the dishpan. One piece of kitchen equipment that did two jobs saved time and money, two resources my grandmother used with care.

My grandmother flung flour about with abandon, not afraid to make a mess since it would be simple to clean up once the job was done right. Rich milk from their dairy went in right from the bottle, home-churned butter from the crock, fresh eggs from a basket on the counter, sugar scooped from a canister—all landed in the big bowl without measuring implements of any kind other than eyes and practiced hands. Now I know that's how professional restaurant chefs do much of their work, with confidence born of knowledge and practice, but at the time I didn't think of her as a master cook and baker feeding a crowd. Neither did she. She loved to bake, especially cakes. From her I learned the pleasure of making a little magic happen by transforming the simplest of ingredients into beautiful, inviting cakes, ready to be savored with family and friends.

I started baking at home when I was nine or ten. I still remember the thrill of making something and bringing it out to my family, who, bless them, always crowed with joy and surprise that little me could make such a magnificent cake or pie or pan of brownies or gingerbread. I never thought of cakes as special or particularly Southern, just as something I loved to make and eat.

My professional life in the kitchen began years later, when I started teaching and writing about the food of Thailand, where I had spent three years as a Peace Corps volunteer. Baking and Southern cooking remained part of my life, but not in a conscious way. If we had company, I might make green chicken curry with rice, or Southern fried chicken with corn on the cob. I learned to make spring rolls and dumplings and spicy Thai salads, but I didn't try to learn new Southern dishes. I just kept on doing what I knew how to do.

Since I have had my own children, now ten and fourteen years old, I've been returning to the Southern foods of my childhood more often, partly to share my history with them, and partly because having a family at home means cooking every day, and usually more than once. It also means that lots of cakes need baking, since we have four birthdays a year, plus those of grandparents, sisters, and friends. Not to mention school festivals, covered dish suppers, family reunions, and church dinners, all of which keep me refilling the sugar and flour canisters and wearing out a mixer now and then.

Not only did baking come back to the forefront of my life; I also moved back to where my earliest baking, cooking, and eating took place. Six years ago, we moved from Southern California, where our daughters were born, back to North Carolina, settling down about an hour away from the kitchens of my childhood.

I came back with a new appreciation of my culinary inheritance, and an eagerness to fill in the gaps in my knowledge. Since we moved here, I have enjoyed the chance to take a long, sweet look at Southern food in general and Southern baking in particular. The opportunity to write this book has been an extraordinary and precious gift. I am moved and astounded daily as I read, talk, taste, research, and daydream my way through the subject of Southern cakes. From pound cake to pineapple upside-down cake, and from Lady Baltimore to Mississippi Mud, this has been a hoot, an education, and a very tasty task. Each recipe, each question, each person seems to lead me to another recipe, question, and person, and what a blessing that is. I feel grateful beyond words to know, at this point in my life, in the twenty-first century, how many people are fascinated by, excited over, occupied with, and opinionated about food, just like me.

I invite you to take a little journey through this collection of Southern cakes. Perhaps you will come across some old friends and meet some new neighbors, since the South, like all the world, grows and changes every day, while still remaining essentially its same old self. I hope that while sampling these pages you will remember something about a cake you once ate or a person who once taught you something about cooking and eating and the sacred nature of food.

I hope you bake some of these cakes, or go find someone who will, or become inspired to head off down the kitchen trail toward another culinary destination that captures your particular fancy. I wish you good eating and good conversation all along the way, and the blessing of connecting the good things of the past to the gifts of the present and the possibilities of the future.

BAKING 101

To bake the cakes presented in this book, you don't have to be a Southerner or a professional cook. You don't even need prior experience in the kitchen. All you require are the basic skills and tools of home baking. You can pick up the skills by reading this book and other cookbooks, asking advice from friends and neighbors, watching people cook on television and in cooking classes, and best of all, by getting out a bowl and spoon and learning by doing. Baking is fun and interesting, which is why I have been doing it since I was ten years old.

Cake baking in the South has changed very little in its essential form since the Colonial era. Here are the principles to keep in mind and equipment to have on hand for making the best use of the recipes in this book.

The Basics of Baking Cakes

BEFORE YOU BAKE

Before you begin your cake, heat the oven to the proper temperature, usually 350°F. Next, prepare your pans before you proceed to mix the cake. This way you can move right through the process and get those cakes into the oven pronto.

In most cases, you will prepare the cake pans by greasing and flouring the insides. First, rub softened butter or shortening generously and evenly all over the interior surface of the baking pan you plan to use. Next, add about 1 tablespoon of flour to the pan, and rotate it to scatter the flour so that it adheres evenly over the entire surface. Then invert the pan to release the extra flour. Finally, rap the edge of the pan on the counter or the edge of the sink to knock loose the remaining excess. Your pan will be left with the thinnest film of grease and flour, which will help the pan to release the cake and the cake to let go of the pan, so that your layer comes out easily onto the cooling rack or serving plate after baking. For extra insurance, cut a circle out of waxed paper or kitchen parchment about the same size as the baking pan, and press it into the baking pan bottom to line it. You can buy ready-made rounds of kitchen parchment for most pan sizes (see the Baker's Catalogue and Sur la Table, pages 161 and 162). You could also grease the waxed paper to be extra sure the cakes will come out of the pans easily.

CREAMING THE BUTTER

Most butter cakes begin with the standard step of creaming butter and sugar together. This means combining softened butter with sugar and then stirring them with enough speed and energy to bring these two ingredients with very different textures (one soft and the other gritty and dry) into one fairly smooth, unified substance. This step gives your cake a strong foundation. The butter should be at room temperature, or 65 to 70°F. Take it out of the refrigerator about 1 hour before using to warm up and soften. If you're ready to bake and the butter is cold, cut it into small chunks and leave them out on the counter for 10 to 15 minutes. To cream the butter and sugar well with a mixer, scrape them down into the well of the bowl often as you work.

ADDING THE EGGS

The next step is usually to incorporate the eggs, one at a time, beating or stirring well after you add each one to give the batter a uniform texture and soften it to a rich, thick, luxurious state. Eggs should be at room temperature for baking, so set them out about 1 hour before you plan to bake. If they are cold when you are ready to begin, set them aside in a small bowl of very warm water for about 10 minutes. Separating whites and yolks is easiest when the eggs are cold. But for beating egg whites to their thickest, most billowy peaks, wait until the whites warm up to room temperature.

FOLDING IN THE DRIES AND THE WETS

The intermediate step for preparing the batter is to combine the dry ingredients (flour, baking powder, baking soda, salt, and spices) and the liquid (milk, buttermilk, water, cream, or juice) with the butter-sugar-egg mixture. This task turns the mixture into a bona fide batter, an entity that is fairly thick, smooth, and usually pourable. The flour mixture contains the lifters—the leavening agents of baking powder, or baking soda and salt—that enable the cake to rise as it bakes. These go to work as soon as they meet moisture, so take care to move right on through the process, from bowl to oven, as soon as you have combined the wet and dry ingredients well.

For this job, I prefer a large wooden spoon, a big spatula, or a mixer on its lowest speed. Too much beating at this point can make for a tough cake. Work the batter only enough to incorporate the flour or the liquid you've just added into the existing batter, probably less than a minute each time you add flour or liquid. Add the dries and wets in alternate batches. Here's the plan: Add about one third of the flour mixture to the butter-sugar-egg mixture in the mixing bowl, and stir until the flour barely disappears. Then, add about half the liquid, followed by half of the remaining flour. Next, stir in the remaining liquid, and finally the last batch of flour. Don't go crazy worrying about getting exact proportions; this is just a method for taking it slowly, bringing all the parts together deliberately, evenly, and without delay, into a uniform whole. Get the ingredients in, without beating too long or too hard, and then get the batter into the oven with all possible speed.

CHECKING FOR DONENESS

Most layer cakes will need 20 to 35 minutes in the oven, while pound cakes and fruitcakes will need an hour or more. To get your cake out when it is done, and before it is overdone, pay attention to what you can see, feel, and smell as it bakes. Set a timer for the minimum amount of time suggested, and begin checking the cake at that point. Look for changes in color and texture: Light-colored batters will probably become a pleasing golden brown. If your batter is a dark color, note the change in texture as the cake begins to look solid, dry, and substantial, rather than shiny and wet. The edges of the cake will darken, harden a little, and begin to shrink away from the sides of the pan. Touch the center lightly to see if the cake springs back, or insert a wooden skewer or a toothpick into the center. When you take it out, there should be no wet batter or crumbs clinging to it. If you check the cake too soon, it may collapse. Removing the cake from the oven as soon as it is properly baked is important, so be ready with pot holders for grasping the hot pan, and clear a place to set it down.

GETTING THE CAKE OUT OF THE PAN

Small wire cooling racks used to be standard kitchen equipment, but nowadays they've become a more specialized tool and are found mostly in specialty kitchenware shops. You can get by without them, using a plate instead, but they are very handy. Individual racks for each layer are ideal to facilitate turning out cakes and transferring them with ease and care. A large rack holding two cakes makes a perfect resting place once the cake layers are out of the pans, but it doesn't help with the delicate and crucial first step of turning them out of the pans.

Most cakes need about a 10-minute rest in the pan on a wire cooling rack, or on a folded kitchen towel if that is not an option.

To turn a cake out of the pan, first use a table knife to loosen it, running the knife along the sides of the pan. Then place a wire rack or a plate, top side down, over the cake pan, and flip it over. The cake should plop down gently onto the wire cooling rack; if it doesn't, turn it right side up and work your way around the sides again with a knife. Hold the pan firmly in one hand and boldly smack it sideways against the open palm of your other hand, making a sharp side-to-side motion to coax the cake loose from the pan. Try the upside-down flip with the rack again. If the cake is stuck, but not burnt, cut it just enough to work a spatula under the cake and release it in sections. Use icing to glue it into shape if possible. If not, enjoy it as a shortcake with berries and whipped cream. (If it's wintertime, simmer 2 cups of frozen berries with 2 tablespoons of sugar and 1 tablespoon of water until you have a nice little juicy and chunky sauce.) Let the cakes finish cooling completely on the racks, top side up, before frosting them.

If you would like to have multiple layers, or thinner ones, you can slice your layers in half horizontally. Work slowly and carefully, keeping your eye and mind on the tip of the knife so that you work your way evenly through the cake. This step works best with a chilled cake, since its texture will be firm.

HOW TO STORE CAKES

Once the cake is baked and cooled, you can frost it at once, or store it in the refrigerator or freezer and frost it later. To store baked cakes, wrap each completely cooled layer tightly in waxed paper or plastic wrap or both, and then enclose it in foil or a resealable plastic bag, pushing all the air out of the bag before sealing it. Most cakes can be kept 2 to 3 days in the refrigerator, and up to 3 months in the freezer, if carefully wrapped so they are airtight.

FROSTING: THE FINISHING TOUCH

In most cases, frost cakes only after they are completely cooled. A few recipes specify that you frost or ice them while they are hot. This is usually so that a glaze can penetrate the cake, helping it absorb the flavors. Before you frost a cake, slip strips of kitchen parchment paper underneath the edges of the bottom layer to keep the serving plate clean.

Frosted cakes usually keep 24 hours to 2 days at room temperature. If the frosting or icing is made with milk, cream, cream cheese, eggs, or other fragile ingredients, store the cake, covered, in the refrigerator. Set it out about 1 hour before serving so that it can warm up to room temperature and be at its tasty best. Many cakes are easiest to slice when they are cold, so if you want to cut a cake in advance, chill it first.

Equipment and Tools

Equipment means pans, cooling racks, pot holders, and other items that allow things to happen. Tools are items we use actively to perform particular tasks. They include whisks, wooden spoons, graters, and sifters. The line between the two is fuzzy sometimes, but don't you worry: this won't be on the test. Just know that what follows is a list of baking items that I consider essential in some cases, and desirable in others. There are many more things worth considering, but this is my list to start you off.

Visit local kitchenware stores, where you can examine and compare a variety of equipment. At these shops, you are likely to find staff who love to cook and bake and can help you decide what you need and show you how to use it. The mail-order section at the end of this book (page 161) has sources for those who don't have a local store. A lso, if you check thrift stores now and then, you may find unusual items from old-time kitchens, as well as conventional tools so that you can get what you need while minding your budget.

THE ESSENTIALS

MIXING BOWLS

I recommend you get a set of nested stainless steel bowls, ranging in size from small-enough-for-cereal to big-enough-to-serve-as-a-dishpan. These sets provide you with enough bowls for wets, dries, and various additions to a batter. They equip you for one-bowl cookie doughs, pound cakes, and ambitious fruitcakes, and are useful in other kinds of cooking. They work perfectly as the top of an improvised double boiler. Set one over a pan of simmering water to melt chocolate, stir lemon curd, or beat simple ingredients into a sweet, glossy bowl full of divinity icing. For beauty as well as practical use, ceramic bowls and bowl sets are a lovely addition to your baking shelf. Other mixing bowls are fine, too, but try to have several sizes, including a very large one.

MIXERS

You can get by with an array of wooden spoons and an eggbeater, like my grandmother did, but you are likely to bake more if you have one or both of these types of mixers:

HANDHELD/PORTABLE MIXERS: These work well, and can handle most kitchen jobs. They are especially useful for the task of making classic frostings, such as **Seven Minute Frosting** (page 147), in a double boiler.

STAND MIXERS: These allow you to handle other kitchen and baking tasks while the machine does the heavy lifting.

SPATULAS

I have several sturdy spatulas and use them constantly. Buy good ones, and have at least two.

WOODEN SPOONS

You need two or more wooden spoons. Ideally, have one or two very large spoons for major beating and stirring tasks, and one or two standard-sized spoons for basic stirring. If you don't have big wooden spoons, large plastic or metal cooking spoons will work in most cases.

MEASURING SPOONS

Get good, sturdy ones. I prefer metal spoons, and I love having two sets, one of loose spoons and one set on a ring. I keep mine out on the counter in a jar when I'm baking, along with a supply of butter knives, forks, and spoons; then I'm ready for tasting, stirring, and other little tasks.

MEASURING CUPS

You need liquid and dry measuring cups. Liquid ones have pouring spouts and handles, and allow headroom so that the liquid you've measured won't slosh out before you mix it in. Dry measuring cups have flat tops, so that you can fill them loosely with flour, sugar, or cocoa, and then level them off with a sweep of the flat edge of a butter knife across the top.

POT HOLDERS

Have four, and keep them very handy when you get ready to bake. If they get wet, the heat will penetrate right through them and burn your hand, so try to keep them dry, or take extra care if they get wet.

WIRE COOLING RACKS FOR CAKES

These are *so* useful for cakes, so try to have two or three. Check kitchenware stores to find them. Get square or round ones, big enough to hold one round or square layer cake on each individual rack.

BAKING PANS

Invest in good ones, ideally light in color and on the heavy side. My suggestions for a basic set include two 9-inch round pans, one 8-inch square pan, one 13-by-9-inch pan, one or two 9-by-5-inch loaf pans, and one 10-inch tube pan (a removable bottom and "feet" for elevating a cooling angel food cake are pluses).

WORTHWHILE IF YOU LOVE TO BAKE

OVEN THERMOMETER

I strongly suggest you consider purchasing an oven thermometer, to ensure that you are baking cakes at the proper temperature. Many ovens, including my five-year-old one, are off by 25° to 50°F, a crucial difference in baking. Knowing this, I can adjust my oven's setting to compensate for its flaw. Oven thermometers are reasonably priced and fairly easy to find.

WHISKS AND EGGBEATERS

These help you combine ingredients into a smooth batter. They are also used to incorporate air into egg whites, cream, and batter to make them lighter and add volume. A balloon whisk has a sturdy handle and a pear-shaped multiple-wire business end, which effectively does its job of inflating egg whites, cream, and other liquids. A regular whisk has a more tapered wire business end, which does a fine job of mixing when volume and speed are not essential. A roux whisk has a flat business end, which is perfect for stirring flour, cornstarch, or any other thickener into oil, melted butter, or another liquid over heat on the stove top. I love eggbeaters for their American can-do practicality, and because that is the tool I started with in my grandmother's kitchen.

CANDY THERMOMETER

If you long to master fudge, thick old-timey icings, caramel, and candies, this tool is an essential gem. Get a good one that will anchor firmly to your saucepan and be easily read when steam is rising and things are happening fast.

LONG SERRATED KNIVES

These are excellent for slicing cake layers horizontally in half, as well as for slicing and serving cakes and breads.

SIFTER OR LARGE SIEVE

A sifter is an old-fashioned tool with a mesh bottom that removes lumps from dry ingredients and combines those ingredients as well. Large sieves are often used in Europe, and work beautifully for all sifting tasks.

BOX GRATER AND MICROPLANE/RASP

A box grater grates and shreds coconut, chocolate, and citrus peel for maximum flavor, and also cheese, carrots, potatoes, and more. A Microplane or rasp is best for quickly grating citrus zest and giving it a fine, fluffy texture.

LEMON REAMER AND CITRUS JUICER

I like my wooden reamer for small amounts of juice. When I want to make lemonade or another lemon-intensive treat, I use my glass citrus juicer, which sits on the counter top. It yields plenty of juice and has a little moat in which juice can accumulate.

DOUBLE BOILER

This set of two nesting pans includes a base for holding simmering water and a cooking vessel, which is suspended over the hot water. Use a double boiler to cook delicate mixtures that could easily burn or curdle if cooked directly on the heat, such as meringue-based icings, lemon curd, fudge icings, candy, and sauces.

MORE PANS

For avid bakers I suggest three 8-inch round layer cake pans; three 9-inch round layer cake pans; a 9-inch square pan or two for old-fashioned square layer cakes; a 9-inch springform pan; two 12-cup muffin pans; a jelly-roll pan or quarter-sheet pan (11 by 15 inches); and a large rectangular pan with low sides used for making thin sheet cakes, rolls, and roulades, including *bûche de Noël* and, of course, the underappreciated, versatile, and surprisingly simple **Jelly Roll** (page 46).

Substitutions and Other Useful Information

Sometimes you discover you have run out of a crucial ingredient. Simple solutions can keep you baking rather than giving up or running to the store. For a comprehensive resource on the subject, get a copy of *The Food Substitutions Bible* by David Joachim.

BUTTERMILK AND SOUR MILK

You can make an excellent stand-in for both buttermilk and sour milk thusly: Stir 1 tablespoon of white or cider vinegar, or 1 tablespoon of lemon or lime juice, into 1 cup of whole milk. Stir well, let stand 10 minutes or longer, and voilà—buttermilk's twin. You can also find dehydrated buttermilk powder in some supermarkets, or order it from The Baker's Catalogue (see page 161).

MILK

Keeping a supply of fresh milk sounds so simple, but it's easy to let this slide. Stock up on evaporated milk and dry milk powder. Make room in the pantry and keep at least three cans on hand. Sometimes one must stop and go to the store in mid-recipe, but you shouldn't have to simply because you are out of milk. Reconstituted milk works just fine in almost every recipe.

BUTTER

Buy a lot, especially when it is sale time. Butter freezes very well for up to 6 months. Have some in the fridge and several boxes in the back corner of the freezer, so you are baking-ready 24/7.

SELF-RISING FLOUR

If a recipe calls for self-rising and you have ordinary flour, simply make up what you need using this formula: For every cup of self-rising flour, mix 1 cup of regular, all-purpose flour with 1 teaspoon of baking powder, ½ teaspoon of salt, and a scant ¼ teaspoon of baking soda.

EGG WHITES AND YOLKS

Powdered egg whites work well in some recipes, so keep a container in the pantry to avoid an extra trip to the store. Check the label for details on mixing the egg whites with water to reconstitute (3 tablespoons of water to 1 tablespoon of powdered egg whites is usually about right).

Powdered egg yolks are available as well. Check the label, but expect to mix ¼ cup of powdered egg yolks with 4 teaspoons water.

If you want pasteurized egg yolks, egg whites, and whole eggs, look for them in the refrigerator case near the eggs. Yolks and whites come in small cartons, easy to pour and store. See the labels for information on how to use them in baking and whether they will work, for example, in meringues.

STORING EXTRA EGG WHITES: Making **Lemon Curd** (page 157) means having extra egg whites. Plan to cook **Angel Food Cake** (page 35) or **Seven-Minute Frosting** (page 147), or store them in the refrigerator for 3 days or the freezer for 2 months. Collect leftover egg whites in a jar. If you want to label it and keep track of how many you have, good for you. I myself accumulate them and measure them for use in recipes (see below). Refrigerate egg whites for 3 to 5 days, or freeze them for up to 6 months, tightly sealed in a jar.

One cup of egg whites is equivalent to the whites of approximately 7 large eggs. About 2 cups of whites is equal to the whites of 1 dozen eggs. One egg white is about 3 tablespoons. Don't go crazy here; eggs are nature-made, so "close" is good enough.

STORING EXTRA EGG YOLKS: If you bake an **Angel Food Cake** (page 35), you will have extra egg yolks, perfect for **Lemon Curd** (page 157) or **Boiled Custard** (page 158). To store egg yolks, stir in 1 teaspoon of sugar per yolk to keep the yolk liquid. Cover and refrigerate for 3 days. For measuring purposes, 1 egg yolk is about 1 tablespoon. A cup of egg yolks is equivalent to the yolks of about 14 eggs.

POUND CAKES

A pound cake is the original Southern cake, connecting home cooks in twenty-first-century Atlanta, Mobile, Louisville, and New Orleans with the cooks in Southern kitchens of nearly three hundred years before. Much has changed in the kitchen since Colonial times. For home bakers, stepping into an eighteenth-century kitchen would be like finding oneself on a different planet.

In the Colonial era, cooks made pound cakes as the English did, weighing the ingredients on a kitchen scale. The recipe still works: 1 pound of flour, 1 pound of sugar, 1 pound of butter, and 1 pound of eggs. To be precise, cooks weighed the eggs first, since the natural world abhors precision. If a cook weighed the eggs and then matched the other three ingredients to that weight exactly, she would have a perfectly balanced cake.

Given the mercurial nature of almost every other aspect of the baking process at that time, getting the cake's proportions right meant a great deal to the cook. The oven temperature was measured by testing the heat with one's hand, and the timing by an hourglass or the angle of the sun streaming into the kitchen.

Baking required a lot more energy during Colonial times. The baker had to build and stoke the fire, and have the batter ready when the temperature in the oven was just right. More elbow grease was required to cream the butter and sugar. Today's baker can choose among stand mixers, hand-held mixers, eggbeaters, and whisks to do the job. We have timers, thermometers, and measuring cups to guide us, and stove tops, ovens, and refrigerators to minimize the physical work once required for baking a cake.

In my twenty-first-century kitchen, I love making the classic pound cake on page 20, because it takes me right back to the kitchens of another time. Mrs. Buttross gives measurements in both pounds and cups, a bridge between old ways and new, especially for those who don't own a kitchen scale. Baking powder is absent in her traditional recipe; it came into use in the mid-nineteenth century.

I also love making CREAM CHEESE POUND CAKE (page 26), a modern recipe with a delicious tang, and MISS EDNA FAUST'S BLUE RIBBON POUND CAKE (page 27), a contemporary variation on the Colonial classic. Like the other recipes in this chapter, both produce a simple, elegant cake. They are dignified, as only pound cake can be, and a pure delight to the palate.

All you need for these cakes is a tube pan, ideally one with a 10-inch diameter and a 10- to 12-cup capacity. Loaf pans work, too. Making pound cakes is a fine primer for the standard cake procedure: creaming softened butter with sugar; beating in eggs to make a fluffy, soft mixture; stirring in flour and liquid with a light touch to keep the batter tender; and finishing things off with a bit of vanilla or another flavoring essence. Then put the batter in the oven and await your reward. These cakes draw you right into the sweet circle of Southern baking.

This recipe comes from Mrs. Waddad Habeeb Buttross of Natchez, Mississippi. Her cookbook, *Waddad's Kitchen: Lebanese Zest and Southern Best*, blossomed from a family keepsake collection into a handsome book reflecting both her Lebanese ancestry and her family's deep roots in Mississippi's fertile soil. Fried corn bread and turkey-bone gumbo share the pages with lamb kibbi, fresh pita bread, and homemade feta cheese. A world-class desserts chapter opens with this genuine pound cake, composed of equal weights of butter, sugar, flour, and eggs. Mrs. Buttross's six children say it is excellent, and they are correct.

Waddad Habeeb Buttross's Classic Pound Cake

SERVES 8 TO 10

1 pound (4 sticks) butter, softened

One 1-pound box (about 3⅔ cups) confectioners' sugar

6 eggs

1 pound sifted all-purpose flour (about 4 cups)

1 teaspoon vanilla extract

HEAT THE OVEN to 325°F, and generously grease and flour a 10-inch tube pan, or two 9-by-5-inch loaf pans.

IN A LARGE MIXING BOWL, beat the butter with a mixer at high speed, scraping down the bowl once, until creamy and smooth, about 1 minute. Add the confectioners' sugar and continue beating to combine well, scraping down the bowl often, about 2 minutes. Add the eggs, one at a time, beating just enough each time to mix the egg into the batter.

ADD THE FLOUR and beat at low speed, or stir with a large spoon, until it disappears. Stir in the vanilla, and then scrape the batter into the prepared pan.

BAKE at 325°F for 1 to 1½ hours (55 to 60 minutes for loaf pans), until the cake is golden and springs back when touched lightly in the center, and until a wooden skewer inserted in the center comes out clean.

COOL THE CAKE in the pan on a wire rack or a folded kitchen towel for 10 minutes. Use a table knife to loosen the cake from the sides of the pan. Carefully turn out the cake onto a wire rack or a plate to cool completely, top side up.

This handsome cake has a deep, rich, chocolate flavor without too much sweetness. But if sweet pleases you as it does me, do spread that frosting on top. You could also dust the cake with confectioners' sugar, or serve it with a generous dollop of whipped cream or a big scoop of vanilla ice cream.

Chocolate Pound Cake *with Chocolate-Pecan Frosting*

SERVES 8 TO 10

Chocolate Pound Cake

- 3 cups sifted all-purpose flour
- ½ cup cocoa
- ¾ teaspoon baking powder
- ½ teaspoon salt
- 1 teaspoon vanilla extract
- 1¼ cups evaporated milk
- 1 cup (2 sticks) butter, softened
- ½ cup shortening
- 1½ cups sugar
- 1½ cups light or dark brown sugar
- 5 eggs

Chocolate-Pecan Frosting

- ¼ cup (½ stick) butter
- One 1-ounce square unsweetened chocolate, or 3 tablespoons cocoa
- 1¼ cups confectioners' sugar
- 3 tablespoons milk
- ½ teaspoon vanilla extract
- 1¼ cups chopped pecans

TO MAKE THE CAKE, heat the oven to 325°F. Generously grease and flour a 10-inch tube pan or two 9-by-5-inch loaf pans. Sift the flour, cocoa, baking powder, and salt into a medium bowl, or stir with a fork to mix them well. Stir the vanilla into the evaporated milk.

IN A LARGE BOWL, combine the butter and the shortening and beat well with a mixer at high speed until they form a smooth, fluffy mixture. Add the sugars gradually, beating well to combine them evenly.

ADD THE EGGS one by one, beating well each time. Add about one third of the flour mixture, and then half the milk, beating each time at low speed only until the flour or milk disappears into the batter. Mix in another third of the flour, the rest of the milk, and then the last of the flour in the same way.

SCRAPE THE BATTER into the prepared pan. Bake at 325°F for about 90 minutes (55 to 60 minutes for loaf pans), until the top of the cake is firm and dry, the sides are pulling away from the pan, and a wooden skewer inserted in the center comes out clean.

COOL THE CAKE in the pan on a wire rack or a folded kitchen towel for 15 minutes. Loosen the cake from the pan with a table knife, and turn it out onto a wire rack or a plate to cool completely, top side up.

TO MAKE THE FROSTING, in a small saucepan, combine the butter and the chocolate or cocoa. Cook over medium heat, stirring often, until melted and smooth. Remove from the heat, add the confectioners' sugar, milk, and vanilla, and stir well until the glaze is smooth.

SPREAD THE GLAZE over the cake while it is still warm, or cool to room temperature and use it to ice the top of the cake. Quickly sprinkle the chopped pecans over the frosting on the top of the cake.

I always thought marble cake was a fifties twist on the familiar layer cake, but I was wrong. The custom of swirling two contrasting shades and flavors of batter into a marbled design dates back to the pound cakes of the 1800s. Molasses or another kind of syrup often provided the color and flavor, boosted by a generous hand with spices, which were always freshly ground. The resulting cake is delicious as well as gorgeous. Getting the swirls and whirls just right is an extra pleasure for the cook.

Marble Molasses Pound Cake

SERVES 6 TO 8

- 2 cups sifted all-purpose flour
- 2 teaspoons baking powder
- 1/4 teaspoon salt
- 1/2 cup (1 stick) butter, softened
- 1 cup sugar
- 2 eggs, beaten
- 2/3 cup milk
- 3 tablespoons molasses or pure cane syrup
- 1 teaspoon ground cinnamon
- 1/2 teaspoon ground nutmeg
- 1/2 teaspoon ground cloves

HEAT THE OVEN to 350°F. Generously grease a 9-by-5-inch loaf pan, line the bottom of the pan with waxed or parchment paper, and flour the pan.

COMBINE the flour, baking powder, and salt in a medium bowl, and stir with a fork to mix well.

IN A LARGE BOWL, beat the butter with a mixer at high speed until light and fluffy. Add the sugar and beat to combine the ingredients well. Add the beaten eggs and continue mixing until the mixture is light, fluffy, and smooth, 1 to 2 minutes. Stop several times to scrape down the bowl.

ADD ABOUT A THIRD of the flour mixture, and then about half of the milk, beating at low speed after each addition just long enough to make the flour or the milk disappear into the batter. Mix in another third of the flour, the rest of the milk, and then the last of the flour in the same way.

SCOOP OUT ABOUT A THIRD of the batter into a medium bowl, and add the molasses, cinnamon, nutmeg, and ground cloves. Stir with a wooden spoon or fork to mix everything into the batter well.

QUICKLY ADD BOTH BATTERS to the pan, a few tablespoonfuls at a time, alternating between the plain and spiced batters. Run a table knife through the batter in a figure-eight pattern to swirl the batters together. Bake at 350°F for about 1 hour, until the cake is golden brown and springs back when touched lightly at the center, and until a wooden skewer inserted in the center comes out clean.

COOL THE CAKE in the pan on a wire rack or a folded kitchen towel for about 10 minutes. Use a table knife to loosen the cake from the sides of the pan. Then turn out the cake onto a wire rack or a plate, remove the paper carefully, and cool completely, top side up.

This makes a handsome cake with a luscious caramel color and deep sweet flavor. It's grand plain, but if you want a fancier finish, top it off with a drizzle of **Quick Caramel Glaze** (page 155).

Brown Sugar Pound Cake

SERVES 6 TO 8

- 3 cups all-purpose flour
- ½ teaspoon baking powder
- ¼ teaspoon salt
- 1 teaspoon vanilla extract
- 1 cup milk
- 1½ cups (3 sticks) butter, softened
- One 1-pound box (about 2¾ cups) dark or light brown sugar
- ½ cup sugar
- 5 eggs

HEAT THE OVEN to 325°F. Grease and flour a 10-inch tube pan, or two 9-by-5-inch loaf pans.

COMBINE the flour, baking powder, and salt in a medium bowl and stir with a fork to mix well. Stir the vanilla into the milk and set aside.

IN A LARGE BOWL, beat the butter with a mixer at high speed until light and fluffy. Add the brown sugar in 3 batches, and then add all of the white sugar, beating well after each addition.

ADD THE EGGS, one by one, beating well after each addition. Add half the flour, and then half the milk, beating at low speed only until the flour or milk disappears into the batter. Add in the rest of the flour, and then the remaining milk, in the same way.

QUICKLY SCRAPE THE BATTER into the prepared pan, and bake at 325°F for 1 hour and 10 minutes (55 to 60 minutes for loaf pans), or until the cake is nicely browned at the edges, springs back when touched lightly at the center, and a wooden skewer inserted in the center comes out clean.

COOL THE CAKE in the pan on a wire rack or a folded kitchen towel for 20 to 30 minutes. Loosen the cake from the pan with a table knife, and turn it out onto a wire rack or a plate to cool completely, top side up.

Cream cheese, the star ingredient here, makes a quiet little sensation in this cake shared with me by Suzanne O'Hara of Burlington, North Carolina. It's moist, wonderfully tangy, and particularly easy to make. Set the cream cheese, butter, and eggs out on the counter for about 30 minutes before you mix them up. If you have more than you need, wrap a portion of it well (see page 14), and tuck it away in the freezer for a few weeks. Or wrap up slices to tuck into lunch boxes and briefcases.

Cream Cheese Pound Cake

SERVES 8 TO 10

HEAT THE OVEN to 325°F. Grease and flour a 10-inch tube pan or two 9-by-5-inch loaf pans.

COMBINE the flour, baking powder, and salt together in a medium bowl and stir with a fork to mix well.

COMBINE the softened butter and cream cheese in a large bowl, and beat well with a mixer at medium speed to transform them into a soft, fluffy mixture. Add the sugar and continue beating 2 minutes more, stopping once to scrape down the sides. Add the eggs, one by one, beating after each addition to mix it in well.

ADD THE FLOUR MIXTURE in 3 batches, beating after each addition at low speed only until the flour disappears. Scrape down the bowl 2 or 3 times as you work. Stir in the vanilla, and scrape the batter into the prepared pan.

BAKE at 325°F for 1 hour and 15 minutes (55 to 60 minutes for loaf pans), until the cake is golden brown, pulling away from the sides, and a wooden skewer inserted in the center comes out clean.

COOL THE CAKE in the pan on a wire rack or a folded kitchen towel until it is at room temperature. Then gently loosen the cake from the sides of the pan with a table knife and turn it out onto a cake stand or serving plate, top side up.

- 3 cups all-purpose flour
- 1 teaspoon baking powder
- ¼ teaspoon salt
- 1 cup (2 sticks) butter, softened
- One 8-ounce package (1 cup) cream cheese, softened
- 3 cups sugar
- 6 eggs
- 1 teaspoon vanilla extract

Miss Edna Faust has healing hands. During an energetic lifetime of caring for people professionally as a nurse, she also ministered sweetly to healthy folks with her legendary cakes. Retirement didn't suit her, so she went back to work part-time, and started taking her famous cakes off to the North Carolina State Fair to see how she measured up. The results? Blue ribbons, "best of the best" prizes, and a fountain of gratitude from us lucky ones who got to sample one of her cakes. Miss Edna's recipe and profile are featured in *Hungry for Home: Stories of Food from Across the Carolinas*.

Miss Edna Faust's Blue Ribbon Pound Cake

SERVES 8 TO 10

- 4 cups sifted all-purpose flour
- 1 teaspoon baking powder
- ¼ teaspoon salt
- 1 teaspoon vanilla extract
- 1 cup milk
- 1 cup (2 sticks) butter, softened
- 1 cup shortening
- 3 cups sugar
- 6 eggs

HEAT THE OVEN to 300°F, and grease and flour a 10-inch tube pan. In a medium bowl, sift together the flour, baking powder, and salt, or stir with a fork to mix well. Stir the vanilla into the milk.

IN A LARGE BOWL, combine the butter and the shortening, and beat them together with a mixer at high speed until they are fluffy and smooth, 1 to 2 minutes. Add the sugar and beat to combine the ingredients well. Add the eggs, one at a time, beating well after each addition and stopping to scrape down the bowl now and then.

ADD ABOUT ONE THIRD of the flour mixture, beating at low speed just until the flour disappears into the batter. Add about half the milk, beat it briefly into the batter, and then continue in the same way with another third of the flour, the remaining milk, and the remaining flour.

SCRAPE THE BATTER into the prepared pan. Bake at 300°F for 1½ hours, or until the cake is golden brown and springs back when touched gently in the center, and a wooden skewer inserted in the center comes out clean.

COOL THE CAKE in the pan on a wire rack or a folded kitchen towel until it reaches room temperature. Then gently loosen the sides of the cake from the pan with a table knife, and turn it out onto a cake stand or serving plate, top side up.

Friends of the Eno River, in Durham County, North Carolina, still miss George Pyne, a passionate advocate for returning the river to its natural splendor. Not only did he devote time and energy to protecting the river, he also put his signature bourbon-kissed pound cake out there on the front lines, energizing his fellow Eno-philes at potlucks, fund-raisers, and the annual feast at which the latest Eno calendar was unveiled. His son Milo Pyne shared this recipe so that good memories and inspiration can flow like the Eno wherever people stir up this fine cake. The Pyne family puts great store in giving this cake a good start by creaming the butter and sugar well with a big wooden spoon.

George Pyne's Bourbon Pound Cake

SERVES 6 TO 8

TO MAKE THE CAKE, heat the oven to 325°F, and grease and flour a 10-inch tube pan. Sift the flour and baking powder together 3 times and set aside, or stir with a fork to mix well.

USING A BIG WOODEN SPOON, mash and mix the butter and shortening together in a medium bowl, and when they are well combined, add about 1 cup of the sugar. Use the wooden spoon to mix everything into a thick, smooth mixture.

CONTINUING WITH THE WOODEN SPOON or changing to a mixer on medium speed, add the remaining 2 cups of sugar slowly, stopping now and then to scrape down the bowl and mix well. Add the eggs, one at a time, beating each time to keep the batter smooth.

ADD ABOUT ONE FOURTH of the flour mixture, and beat at low speed just until it disappears. Add about half of the milk, and beat only until smooth. Mix in another fourth of the flour, and then the rest of the milk. Stir in another fourth of the flour, then the bourbon, and finally the remaining flour, beating each time just enough to keep the batter smooth. Stir in the vanilla, and scrape the batter into the prepared pan.

BAKE at 325°F for 60 to 70 minutes, or until the cake is golden brown, springs back when touched lightly in the center, and a wooden skewer inserted in the center comes out clean. Place the cake, in the pan, on a wire rack or a folded kitchen towel to cool completely before icing. Gently loosen the cake from the sides of the pan and turn it out onto a cake stand or serving plate, top side up.

Bourbon Pound Cake

- 3 cups sifted all-purpose flour
- 2 teaspoons baking powder
- 1 cup (2 sticks) butter, softened
- 1/3 cup shortening
- 3 cups sugar
- 5 eggs
- 1 3/4 cups milk
- 1/4 cup bourbon or apple cider
- 2 teaspoons vanilla extract

Bourbon Icing

- One 8-ounce package (1 cup) cream cheese, softened
- ½ cup (1 stick) butter, softened
- One 1-pound box (3⅔ cups) confectioners' sugar
- ¼ cup bourbon or apple cider
- 1 teaspoon vanilla extract

TO MAKE THE ICING, in a medium bowl, combine the cream cheese and butter, and use a wooden spoon or another large spoon to mix them together well. Add about one fourth of the confectioners' sugar, and use the spoon to mash and mix it in well.

USING A MIXER, add another fourth of the confectioners' sugar and beat at medium speed until it is mixed in evenly. Add half the bourbon and mix well, then another fourth of the sugar and mix well again, stopping to scrape down the sides of the bowl. Mix in the remaining bourbon, and then the last of the sugar and the vanilla. When the frosting is smooth, cover and chill well before using, 40 minutes or more.

SPREAD THE COLD ICING over the cake, applying it first to the sides, then up over the top. Chill the cake before serving, so that the icing hardens.

I adore this cake, which bakes up tall, aromatic with spices, and fortified with the autumnal rosy-golden color and comforting flavor of sweet potatoes. If you long for a little pizzazz, top this off with **Buttermilk Glaze** (see page 117) or **Quick Caramel Glaze** (page 155). All pound cakes taste sublime when toasted, but this one blesses you with its spicy aroma as well.

Sweet Potato Pound Cake

SERVES 8 TO 10

3¼ cups sifted all-purpose flour
2 teaspoons baking powder
½ teaspoon baking soda
½ teaspoon ground nutmeg
½ teaspoon salt
½ cup milk
1 teaspoon vanilla extract
1 cup (2 sticks) butter, softened
1 cup sugar
1 cup light brown sugar
4 eggs
2 cups mashed cooked sweet potatoes

HEAT THE OVEN to 350°F, and grease and flour a 10-inch tube pan. Combine the flour, baking powder, baking soda, nutmeg, and salt in a medium bowl, and stir with a fork to mix well. Combine the milk and vanilla in a small bowl. Set the milk and flour mixtures aside.

IN A LARGE BOWL, beat the butter, sugar, and brown sugar together with a mixer at high speed until light and well combined, stopping once or twice to scrape down the bowl. Add the eggs, one at a time, beating well each time. Add the mashed sweet potatoes and mix at low speed for 1 minute, or until the batter is evenly mixed.

ADD ABOUT HALF the flour mixture and beat gently, using a wooden spoon or a mixer at low speed, only until the flour disappears into the batter. Add half the milk and mix gently to combine everything well. Mix in the remaining flour, and then the remaining milk, beating gently only until you have a thick, smooth batter.

SCRAPE THE BATTER into the prepared tube pan, and bake at 350°F for between 60 and 75 minutes, or until the cake is evenly browned, springs back when touched gently in the center, and a wooden skewer inserted in the center comes out clean.

COOL IN THE PAN on a wire rack or a folded kitchen towel for 20 minutes. Then use a table knife to loosen the cake from the pan. Turn out the cake onto a wire rack, place it top side up, and cool to room temperature.

ANTIQUES AND HEIRLOOMS

These cakes are family treasures, passed down from the old folks to the new generation, time and again. They have survived partly because they connect us to the past and partly because they look so pretty and taste so good. Each generation takes care to keep them in the family, but unlike Aunt Estelle's cameo or the family silver, we also share them easily and often with friends and neighbors, who might just adapt them into a family treasure of their own. Antiques have value not simply because they are old, but because they show us connections and nourish our souls.

These cakes take us back to times gone by, to cooks in Colonial Virginia and the Mississippi Delta, to a turn-of-the-century tearoom in Charleston, South Carolina, and the Tuskegee Institute in Mobile, Alabama. LANE CAKE (page 38) shows up in Harper Lee's extraordinary novel *To Kill a Mockingbird*, while LUBA TOOTER COHEN'S BABKA (page 51) connects Jewish Southerners in Arkansas to their roots in turn-of-the-century Russia. Many recipes were created by cooks who beat their egg whites by hand on a platter with a flat whisk and baked in ovens heated with chunks of wood.

Bake these cakes with a sense of history, but choose those that you think will delight your family and friends. And let this chapter be a reminder to explore your own family's culinary history. Find out what your people cooked and ate two or three generations back, either by talking with relatives or by exploring historical works. Write down the stories that go with the dishes, so that those who come along later will have a recipe box to connect them right back to you.

These small, elegant tea cakes were enjoyed in Virginia homes during Colonial times. Popular long before baking soda and baking powder debuted in the kitchens of the mid-nineteenth century, queen cakes depend on well-beaten eggs to make them rise, just as pound cakes do. Their texture is dense, closer to a delicate corn bread than to today's muffins and cupcakes. This recipe comes from my daughter's bookshelf. It was reproduced in *Felicity's Cookbook*, edited by Polly Athan and Jodi Evert, a beautifully illustrated collection of early American recipes published by American Girl in 1994. For rosewater and orange flower water, see the sources at the back of the book (page 161) or look in Middle Eastern markets.

Colonial Queen Cakes

SERVES 24

1 cup all-purpose flour

1/4 teaspoon salt

1/4 teaspoon ground mace or nutmeg

1/4 cup currants or raisins

1/2 cup (1 stick) butter, softened

1/2 cup sugar

2 eggs

2 tablespoons rosewater or orange flower water, or
1 teaspoon vanilla extract

HEAT THE OVEN to 325°F, and grease and lightly flour two 12-cup muffin pans. (Don't use paper muffin cups—these small cakes work best cooked right in the pan.)

COMBINE the flour, salt, and mace in a medium bowl, and stir with a fork to mix well. Stir in the currants or raisins, breaking up any clumps, so that they are coated with flour.

IN A LARGE BOWL, stir the butter with a wooden spoon until smooth. Add the sugar, pressing and scraping with a wooden spoon or a spatula to combine them well. Add the eggs, one by one, mixing well each time, until the batter is thick and smooth. Stir in the rosewater, and then add the flour mixture, stirring only enough to make the flour disappear into the batter.

DIVIDE THE BATTER quickly among the muffin cups: First spoon only a tablespoonful of batter into each cup, and then divide the remaining batter among the cups. Bake at 325°F for 15 to 20 minutes, until the little cakes are golden around the edges, and rounded, firm, and shiny on top. Let stand for 5 minutes, and then carefully loosen the cakes with a table knife and transfer them to a wire rack or a folded kitchen towel to cool completely.

This cake rises up to heaven on the glory of well-beaten egg whites alone. No boost from baking powder or baking soda here. You can use a balloon whisk, as folks did before electricity lit up the kitchen, or use an electric mixer and see how quickly a genuine heirloom dessert can be baking away in your oven. Resist the urge to grease the tube pan. Angel food cake needs traction on the walls of the pan in order to rise.

Angel Food Cake

SERVES 8 TO 10

1¼ cups sifted cake flour
¼ teaspoon salt
1½ cups sugar
1½ cups egg whites (10 to 12)
1¼ teaspoons cream of tartar
1 teaspoon vanilla extract

HEAT THE OVEN to 325°F. Set out a 10-inch tube pan, but do not grease it.

SIFT the flour, salt, and ½ cup of the sugar into a small bowl, or combine them and stir with a fork to mix well.

BEAT THE EGG WHITES with a mixer at medium speed in a medium bowl until pale yellow and very bubbly. Add the cream of tartar, and continue beating until the egg whites swell into thick, velvety clouds. While still beating, sprinkle in the remaining 1 cup of sugar by spoonfuls, scraping down the bowl often, and beat until the egg whites have a soft, substantial shape and hold curled peaks. Beat in the vanilla.

FINISH THE BATTER by carefully folding in the flour mixture in four batches. Use a rubber spatula or a large wooden spoon, folding gently each time only until the flour barely disappears.

QUICKLY SCRAPE THE BATTER into the ungreased tube pan, and then run a table knife through the center of the batter, going all the way around the tube, to break up any large air pockets. Bake at 325°F for 40 to 45 minutes, until golden brown and fairly firm in the center.

REMOVE THE CAKE from the oven and turn it upside down over a wine bottle or another tall, slender glass bottle; or balance it on the metal extensions protruding from the pan for this very purpose, if you have such a pan. Let your angel food cake stand upside down until it is completely cool, 1 hour or more.

TO REMOVE THE CAKE from the pan, gently run a table knife around the sides of the cake, loosening it from the pan. Turn out the cake on a cake plate or cake stand, top side up. With a serrated knife, use a gentle, sawing motion to cut the cake, or pull the cake into thick slices using two forks.

Growing up in the Mississippi Delta, Kathy Starr learned more than recipes from her grandmother, Miz Bob, whose culinary memories stretched back three generations, to the time of the Civil War. Miz Bob raised children and grandchildren and ran a thriving café. She instilled in her granddaughter a pride in her people and her place in the world, and a joy in cooking for family and friends. Ms. Starr's extraordinary culinary memoir, *The Soul of Southern Cooking*, includes this recipe for a classic jelly cake, a yellow cake filled with jelly or jam between its layers and iced with more on the top. Ms. Starr stirs confectioners' sugar into berry jelly for a ravishing jewel color on a simply charming cake.

Kathy Starr's

Mississippi Delta Jelly Cake

SERVES 8 TO 10

1 teaspoon salt

3⅓ cups sifted flour, preferably cake flour

Dash of baking soda

1½ teaspoons baking powder

1 cup (2 sticks) plus 1 teaspoon butter, softened

2⅔ cup sugar

½ cup vegetable oil

4 eggs, beaten

1 cup milk

¾ cup confectioners' sugar

1½ cups (one 12-ounce jar) strawberry jelly, or blackberry or raspberry jam

HEAT THE OVEN to 325°F, and grease and flour three 8-inch or two 9-inch round cake pans.

COMBINE THE SALT with about 2⅔ cups of the flour in a medium bowl, and stir with a fork to mix well. Combine the baking soda, baking powder, and the remaining ⅔ cup of flour in a small bowl, and stir well.

CREAM THE BUTTER, sugar, and oil with a mixer at medium speed until creamy, with no gritty signs of sugar. Add the eggs, beating for 1 to 2 minutes. Stir in the flour-salt mixture in 3 batches, alternating with the milk. Gently fold in the flour–baking soda–baking powder mixture, and stir just until the flour disappears.

POUR INTO THE PREPARED PANS. Bake at 325°F for 25 to 30 minutes, until the cake is golden brown and springs back when touched lightly in the center. Cool in the pans on a wire rack or a folded kitchen towel for 10 minutes. Then turn the cakes out onto wire racks or plates, and place them top side up to cool completely.

TO FINISH THE CAKE, combine the confectioners' sugar and jelly in a medium bowl and stir with a fork until all the lumps disappear. Place one layer, top side down, on a serving plate or a cake stand, and spread a third of the jelly icing over it thickly. Repeat with the second layer. Place the final layer on the cake, top side up, and ice it with the remaining jelly icing. Do not ice the sides of the cake.

Mrs. Emma Rylander Lane of Clayton, Alabama, included this recipe, which she called her prize cake, in a small cookbook she self-published in 1898. She used only chopped raisins in the filling, but later versions typically include shredded coconut and pecans as well. Some people love the filling so much that they make extra and use it to ice the entire cake. I use the coconut-pecan variation in my filling recipe and cover the cake with that sweet, fluffy, old-time white frosting, just like Mrs. Lane did. Save extra egg whites in your freezer for your next **Angel Food Cake** (page 35). If possible, make your Lane Cake a day in advance.

Lane Cake

SERVES 6 TO 8

TO MAKE THE CAKE, heat the oven to 350°F. Prepare three 9-inch cake pans, or three 8-inch pans, greasing them well, lining them with circles of waxed paper or kitchen parchment, and dusting them with a little flour. Sift the flour, baking powder, and salt into a medium bowl, or stir with a fork to mix well. Stir the vanilla into the milk.

IN ANOTHER MEDIUM BOWL, beat the egg whites with a mixer at medium speed for about 1 minute, until they are foamy and pale yellow. Increase the speed to high, and beat the egg whites until they swell into white, soft clouds, and hold a firm, curled peak when you lift the beaters out. Set aside.

COMBINE the butter and sugar together in a large bowl and beat with the mixer at high speed until they are fluffy and well combined, stopping once or twice to scrape down the bowl. Add the flour and the milk in thirds, alternating between the two and beating at low speed after each addition only until the flour or milk disappears and the batter is smooth.

ADD about one third of the beaten egg whites to the batter, using a wooden spoon or a spatula to fold them in gently. Fold in the remaining egg whites, mixing everything gently only until well combined.

QUICKLY DIVIDE THE BATTER among the prepared pans and bake at 350°F for 20 to 25 minutes until the cakes are a pale golden brown, spring back when touched lightly in the center, and begin to pull away from the sides of the pans.

COOL IN THE PANS for 10 minutes on wire racks or folded kitchen towels. Then turn out the cakes onto wire racks or plates, carefully remove the waxed paper from the bottoms, and turn the cakes top side up to cool completely.

TO MAKE THE FILLING, in a medium bowl, combine the egg yolks and the sugar. Beat well with a mixer at medium speed for 4 to 5 minutes, until they are thick, billowy, and pale yellow. Transfer to a medium saucepan, add the butter, and then cook over medium

Cake

- 3¼ cups all-purpose flour
- 1 tablespoon baking powder
- ½ teaspoon salt
- 1 teaspoon vanilla extract
- 1 cup milk
- 8 egg whites
- 1 cup (2 sticks) butter, softened
- 2 cups sugar

Filling

8 egg yolks

1¼ cups sugar

½ cup (1 stick) butter

1 cup shredded coconut

1 cup chopped raisins

1 cup chopped pecans

⅓ cup bourbon, apple cider or juice, or orange juice

1 teaspoon vanilla extract

⅛ teaspoon salt

Fluffy White Frosting

¾ cup sugar

2 egg whites

3 tablespoons water

1 tablespoon corn syrup

⅛ teaspoon salt

¾ teaspoon vanilla extract

heat, stirring often and well, until thickened and smooth, 15 to 20 minutes. The filling should coat the back of a spoon and reach a temperature of 160°F on a candy thermometer. Remove from the heat and stir in the coconut, chopped raisins and pecans, bourbon, vanilla, and salt. Stir well to mix everything together into a uniformly thick, chunky filling. Cool to room temperature, and spread between the layers of the cake. Or cool, cover, and refrigerate the filling until ready to use.

TO MAKE THE FROSTING, bring about 3 inches of water to a boil in a medium saucepan or in the bottom of a double boiler. Meanwhile, combine the sugar, egg whites, water, corn syrup, and salt in a large heat-proof bowl that will fit snugly over the saucepan, or in the top of the double boiler. Beat for 1 minute with a mixer at low speed, until the egg white mixture is foamy and well combined.

PLACE THE MIXING BOWL or the double boiler top over the pan of boiling water, and adjust the heat to maintain a gentle boil. Using a hand-held electric mixer at high speed, beat the sugar–egg white mixture at high speed for 7 to 14 minutes, until it swells into a voluptuous cloud of icing that holds firm, curly peaks when the beaters are lifted. Remove from the heat, add the vanilla, and beat for 2 minutes more, scraping down the bowl once or twice.

SPREAD THE FROSTING on the sides and top of the cake. If possible, let stand for several hours while the cake sets and mellows into a state of ripe confectionery perfection.

My cousin Libbie Hall shared her family's recipe for the queen of Southern cake extravaganzas, Lady Baltimore. Her father, Thaddeus Hall, came to North Carolina from Tennessee as a young man to study at Duke University. He stayed on to marry my aunt, and to serve for many years as a beloved principal in the Durham city schools. His sisters shared this Hall family recipe with Libbie's mother, Mary Elizabeth Suitt Hall, so that she could keep this magnificent cake a part of the Hall family celebrations. Gorgeous and delicious, this cake is reason enough for you to invest in a pedestal cake stand if you don't have one already.

Lady Baltimore Cake

SERVES 6 TO 8

Filling

- ½ cup golden or dark raisins
- ½ cup finely chopped dried figs, apricots, cranberries, or dates
- ½ cup finely chopped pecans or walnuts
- 2 tablespoons brandy, sherry, orange juice, or grape juice

Royal Three-Layer White Cake

- 2 cups sifted all-purpose flour
- 2 teaspoons baking powder
- ½ teaspoon salt
- 1 teaspoon vanilla extract
- 1 cup milk
- 4 egg whites
- 1½ cups sugar
- ½ cup (1 stick) butter or shortening, softened

TO MAKE THE FILLING, in a small bowl, combine the raisins, figs, and pecans, and toss to mix well. Add the brandy or juice and toss to mix well. Set aside for 1 hour, or up to 1 day.

TO MAKE THE CAKE, heat the oven to 350°F. Grease three 8-inch or 9-inch round cake pans, line each one with a circle of waxed paper or parchment, and flour the pans. In a medium bowl, combine the flour, baking powder, and salt, and stir with a fork to mix well. Add the vanilla to the milk and set both mixtures aside.

IN ANOTHER MEDIUM BOWL, beat the egg whites with a mixer at low speed until foamy, and then beat at medium-high speed until they become shiny, thick, and stiff, but not dry.

IN A LARGE BOWL, cream the sugar and butter with a mixer at high speed until light and fluffy, stopping to scrape down the sides of the bowl now and then. Reduce the mixer's speed to low, and carefully pour in the milk-vanilla mixture, beating only until blended.

ADD THE FLOUR MIXTURE to the batter all at once, and beat at low speed only until the flour disappears. Add half the egg whites, folding gently with a rubber spatula or a large spoon until they are mixed well into the batter. Fold in the remaining egg whites gently, and then quickly divide the batter among the 3 cake pans.

BAKE at 350°F for 25 minutes, or until the cakes are golden, spring back when touched gently in the center, and begin to pull away from the sides of the pans.

LET THE CAKES COOL in the pans for 5 minutes on wire racks or folded kitchen towels. Then turn out the cakes onto wire racks or plates, carefully remove the waxed paper from the bottoms, and turn the cakes top side up to cool completely.

CONTINUED

CONTINUED

TO MAKE THE ICING, bring about 3 inches of water to a boil in a medium saucepan or in the bottom of a double boiler. Meanwhile, combine the sugar, egg whites, corn syrup, salt, and cream of tartar in a large, heat-proof bowl that will fit snugly over the saucepan, or in the top of the double boiler. Beat for 1 minute with a mixer at low speed, until the mixture is foamy and well combined.

PLACE THE MIXING BOWL or the double boiler top over the pan of boiling water, and adjust the heat to maintain a gentle boil. Using a hand-held electric mixer, beat the sugar–egg white mixture at high speed for 7 to 14 minutes, until it swells into a voluptuous cloud of icing that holds firm, curly peaks when the beaters are lifted. Remove from the heat, add the vanilla, and beat for 2 minutes more, scraping down the bowl once or twice.

TO COMPLETE THE FILLING, scoop about 1½ cups of the icing into a medium bowl, and stir in the dried fruits and nuts, juice and all. Mix well and set aside.

TO COMPLETE THE CAKE, place one layer on a serving plate, top side down, and scoop half the filling onto the cake. Spread the filling over the cake layer, making it a bit thicker around the edges. Cover with a second cake layer, top side down, and spread the remaining filling the same way.

PLACE THE THIRD CAKE LAYER on the second one, top side up, and then cover the entire cake with the remaining icing, spreading it evenly over the sides and then the top. Use a table knife to swirl the icing into beautiful peaks and curls.

Icing

- 1 cup sugar
- 2 egg whites
- ¼ cup light corn syrup
- ¼ teaspoon salt
- ¼ teaspoon cream of tartar
- 1 teaspoon vanilla extract

This simple recipe produces an extraordinary and unusual little confection that inspired **Huguenot Torte** (page 101), one of Charleston's signature cakes. John and Ann Egerton, authors of *Southern Food: At Home, On the Road, In History*, traced this dessert to Henrietta Stanley Dull's apple torte, which appeared in her landmark book *Southern Cooking*, published in Atlanta in 1928. Mrs. Dull's apple torte seems the likely inspiration for the many Ozark pudding recipes out there, but how and why this dish absconded to the Ozarks and changed its name from "torte" to "pudding" is a mystery for another day. One thing is clear: Ozark pudding is easy to make and delicious warm or at room temperature.

Ozark Pudding

SERVES 8 TO 10

¼ cup all-purpose flour

1½ teaspoons baking powder

¼ teaspoon salt

2 eggs

1 teaspoon vanilla extract

1 cup sugar

1 cup finely chopped pecans or walnuts

1 cup finely chopped firm, tart apples

Sweetened whipped cream (optional)

HEAT THE OVEN to 350°F. Generously grease an 8-by-12-inch biscuit pan, a 9-inch square pan, or an 8-inch square or round cake pan.

COMBINE the flour, baking powder, and salt in a small bowl, and stir with a fork to mix well.

IN A MEDIUM BOWL, beat the eggs very well with a mixer at high speed until they become pale yellow, smooth, and thick. Add the vanilla, and then add the sugar in 3 batches, beating well each time and scraping down the bowl often. Sprinkle on the flour mixture, and stir it in with a big spoon only until the flour disappears. Sprinkle the nuts over the batter, and then the apples. Fold them gently into the batter, just until evenly mixed.

SCRAPE THE BATTER into the prepared pan and bake at 350°F for 25 to 30 minutes, until the torte is puffed, golden brown, and pulling away from the sides of the pan. Place on a wire rack or a folded kitchen towel and cool completely in the pan. To serve, cut into squares and use a spatula to carefully transfer them to serving plates. The torte will be dry, crusty, and crumbly on top, and completely delicious. Serve warm or at room temperature, with a generous cloud of sweetened whipped cream if you like.

History books tell us that Dr. Carver was a brilliant research scientist and a dedicated teacher. From Catherine Quick Tillery's extraordinary book *The African-American Heritage Cookbook: Traditional Recipes and Fond Remembrances from Alabama's Renowned Tuskegee Institute*, I learned that recipes played a role in his economic development efforts on behalf of farmers in Macon County, Alabama, in the 1920s. To encourage local farmers to cultivate peanuts as a means to nourish their soil, generate a cash crop, and improve nutrition, he sent out bulletins filled with recipes for soups, breads, vegetarian protein dishes, candies galore, and of course, cakes.

Dr. George Washington Carver's Metropolitan Cake with Peanuts

SERVES 8 TO 10

This one includes peanuts in both the cake layers and the icing. I've adapted the recipe from *Dr. Carver's Agricultural Bulletin no. 31*, "How to Grow the Peanut and 105 Ways of Preparing It for Human Consumption," published around 1925. I've omitted the candied citron that he includes with the peanuts in the batter, and replaced the egg whites with whole eggs, both for color and texture. **Blanche's Never-Fail Chocolate Icing** (page 154) works wonderfully with this cake, as does Kathy Starr's jelly icing (page 37).

Dr. Carver's Metropolitan Peanut Cake

- 2½ cups well-sifted all purpose flour
- 2 teaspoons baking powder
- 1 cup finely chopped roasted and salted peanuts
- 1½ cups (3 sticks) butter, softened
- 1 cup sugar
- 2 eggs
- ½ cup milk

TO MAKE THE CAKE, heat the oven to 350°F, and generously grease and flour two 9-inch layer cake pans. Combine the flour, baking powder, and chopped peanuts in a medium bowl, and stir with a fork to mix well.

CREAM THE BUTTER and sugar in a medium bowl, beating at high speed with a mixer until they are light and well mixed. Add the eggs and beat well until thick, smooth, and fluffy. Add half the flour mixture and beat at low speed until it disappears into the batter. Add the milk and beat just enough to mix it in. Add the remaining flour and stir it in with a spoon or spatula.

DIVIDE THE BATTER between the prepared pans, and bake at 350°F for 25 to 30 minutes, until the cakes are golden brown, spring back when touched lightly in the center, and begin to pull away from the sides of the pans. Cool the cakes in the pans on wire racks or folded kitchen towels for 10 minutes. Then turn out the cakes onto wire racks or plates and cool, top side up.

TO MAKE THE PASTRY CREAM, in a small bowl, combine the sugar and the cornstarch and use a fork to mix them together well.

Dr. Carver's Peanut Pastry Cream

- 2 cups sugar
- 3 tablespoons cornstarch
- 3 cups milk
- 2 cups finely chopped roasted and salted peanuts
- 1 tablespoon butter
- 2 teaspoons lemon or vanilla extract
- Finely chopped roasted and salted peanuts for sprinkling (optional)

IN A MEDIUM SAUCEPAN, combine the milk and the chopped peanuts and place over medium heat. Bring to a gentle boil, adjust the heat to maintain a gentle simmer, and cook for 5 minutes. Stir in the sugar mixture, bring back to a gentle boil, and cook for about 3 minutes more, stirring often, until thickened and smooth. Remove from the heat, and stir in the butter and lemon extract. Cool to room temperature, stirring now and then.

TO FINISH THE CAKE, place one layer, top side down, on a serving plate, and cover it evenly with half of the pastry cream. Place the second layer on the first one, top side up, and cover it with the remaining pastry cream. Leave the sides plain. If you like, sprinkle the top with finely chopped peanuts.

This old-fashioned confection is remarkable for how delightful it is to see and to eat, how seldom we see it nowadays, and how simple it is to make. The cake is delicate and airy, quickly mixed up, and baked in a flash. The filling can be jelly, including good old grape jelly from the peanut-butter-and-jelly shelf, or raspberry jam or **Lemon Curd** (page 157), or a batch of firmly whipped cream sweetened with confectioners' sugar and a dollop of blackberry jam. You need a particular pan here: either a long and shallow rectangle with 1-inch-high sides known as a jelly-roll pan, or a quarter-sheet pan. Anything with low sides in the 11-by-15-inch range will work. This size pan makes a good cookie sheet and sheet-cake pan. Once you get the hang of this lovely cake, you will get lots of use out of it making jelly rolls.

Jelly Roll

SERVES 8 TO 10

- 1 cup all-purpose flour
- 3/4 teaspoon baking powder
- 1/4 teaspoon salt
- 1 cup confectioners' sugar for dusting the cloth (optional)
- 4 eggs
- 1 cup sugar
- 2 tablespoons water
- 1 teaspoon vanilla extract
- 1 cup blackberry or raspberry jam, currant jelly, **Lemon Curd** (page 157), or sweetened whipped cream flavored with jam

HEAT THE OVEN to 400°F and generously grease an 11-by-15-inch jelly-roll pan. Line the pan with waxed paper or kitchen parchment and grease it as well.

COMBINE the flour, baking powder, and salt in a medium bowl, and stir with a fork to mix well. Place a fresh kitchen towel on the countertop with a long side toward you, and sprinkle the towel generously and evenly with the confectioners' sugar.

IN A MEDIUM BOWL, beat the eggs at high speed with a mixer until bright yellow and thickened, about 2 minutes. Add the sugar gradually, beating as you go, and continue beating for 3 to 4 minutes, until pale yellow, velvety, and thick. Add the water and vanilla to the bowl, and beat for 1 minute to mix them in well. Set the mixer aside and finish the cake by hand.

SPRINKLE THE FLOUR MIXTURE over the batter, and then mix it in gently with a wooden spoon or a rubber spatula. Scrape the batter into the prepared pan, and spread it out to form a smooth layer.

BAKE at 400°F for 8 to 10 minutes, until the cake is browned at the edges and springs back when touched lightly at the center. Remove from the oven and quickly turn out onto the prepared kitchen towel. Peel away the waxed paper, then carefully roll up the cake, lifting the long side nearest you, and folding in the towel with the cake.

LET THE ROLLED-UP CAKE COOL for about 15 minutes, and then carefully unroll. Spread the inside with the 1 cup of jam or jelly, extending it almost to the edges, but not quite. Roll the cake back up tightly, and place it on the towel, seam side down, to cool and set.

JUST BEFORE SERVING, sprinkle the cake with a little confectioners' sugar if you like. Then transfer to a serving plate, or wrap tightly and refrigerate if not serving within 2 hours. Set out in advance of serving, about an hour, to return to room temperature.

Unlike caramel cake, which is a yellow or white cake with a thick caramel frosting, a burnt sugar cake has caramel inside and out. Step one is to caramelize sugar into a robust amber syrup, and step two is to enjoy its flavor and color in both the cake and the frosting. Though it strikes me as a cake from the mid-nineteenth century, our national culinary treasure Jean Anderson traces it only as far back as the 1930s in her landmark *American Century Cookbook*. You can make the syrup in advance and have it handy for future cakes, or for infusing caramel lusciousness into a mug of warm milk at bedtime on a wintry evening.

Burnt Sugar Cake

SERVES 6 TO 8

Burnt Sugar Syrup

- 1 cup sugar
- 1 cup boiling water

Burnt Sugar Cake

- 3 cups all-purpose flour
- 1 tablespoon baking powder
- ½ teaspoon salt
- 1 teaspoon vanilla extract
- 1 cup milk
- 1 cup (2 sticks) butter, softened
- 1¾ cups sugar
- 4 eggs

TO MAKE THE SYRUP, heat the sugar in a cast-iron skillet, or in another heavy pan with a broad bottom and high sides, over medium-low heat, stirring occasionally, until the sugar melts into a clear, brown caramel syrup, about the color of tea. Carefully add the boiling water, pouring it down the side of the pan so that if the syrup foams and bubbles up, you'll be protected. Continue cooking, stirring often, until the water joins the caramel in a handsome brown syrup. Remove from the heat and set aside to cool. Store the cooled syrup in a sealed jar until needed.

TO MAKE THE CAKE, heat the oven to 350°F. Grease and flour two 9-inch round cake pans. In a medium bowl, combine the flour, baking powder, and salt, and stir with a fork to mix well. Stir the vanilla into the milk.

IN A LARGE BOWL, beat the butter and the sugar with a mixer at high speed for 2 to 3 minutes, until they are very well combined, stopping now and then to scrape down the bowl. Add the eggs, one by one, beating well each time. Pour in ½ cup of the Burnt Sugar Syrup, and beat well. Add about a third of the flour mixture, and then about half of the milk, beating at low speed just long enough, after each addition, to make the flour or the milk disappear into the batter. Mix in another third of the flour, the rest of the milk, and then the last of the flour in the same way.

DIVIDE THE BATTER between the cake pans and bake at 350°F for 20 to 25 minutes, until the cakes are golden brown, spring back when touched gently in the center, and begin to pull away from the sides of the pans. Let the cakes cool in the pans on wire racks or folded kitchen towels for 15 minutes. Then turn out the cakes onto wire racks or plates to cool completely, top side up.

Burnt Sugar Frosting

- 3¾ cups confectioners' sugar
- ½ cup Burnt Sugar Syrup
- ¼ cup (½ stick) butter, softened
- ½ teaspoon vanilla extract
- 2 to 3 tablespoons evaporated milk or milk

TO MAKE THE FROSTING, in a large bowl, combine the confectioners' sugar, the remaining ½ cup of the Burnt Sugar Syrup, the butter, and the vanilla. Beat with a mixer at medium speed for 2 to 3 minutes, scraping down the bowl now and then to bring the ingredients together. Add 2 tablespoons of evaporated milk and continue beating until the frosting is thick, soft, smooth, and easy to spread. Add a little more sugar if it is thin, and a little more evaporated milk if it seems too thick.

TO COMPLETE THE CAKE, place one layer, top side down, on a cake stand or serving plate, and scoop about ¾ cup of the frosting onto the cake. Spread to the edges and place the second layer over it, top side up. Frost the sides of the cake, and then the top, covering it evenly.

Born in Odessa, Russia, Luba Tooter immigrated to America with her family as a young girl in 1913. Marriage to Jimmy Cohen took her from New York City to Blytheville, Arkansas, where she raised a family, weaving her European Jewish heritage into her Southern American Jewish life. Did she arrive in America clutching this Old World coffee cake recipe in her hand? Not exactly. She learned it from her daughter-in-law, Huddy Horowitz Cohen, in the 1950s. Her granddaughter, Marcie Cohen Ferris, illuminates the world of Jewish Southerners in *Matzoh Ball Gumbo: Culinary Tales of the Jewish South.* The yeast dough for this coffee cake is a soft, stirred-up batter. The pillowy lift of yeast without any elbow grease—very nice.

Luba Tooter Cohen's Babka

SERVES 8 TO 10

Babka

- 1 cup milk, heated until warm but not hot
- One 1/4-ounce package active dry yeast (about 1 tablespoon), or one 3/5-ounce cake compressed yeast
- 1/4 teaspoon salt
- 1/2 cup sugar
- 3 1/2 cups all-purpose flour
- 1/2 cup raisins
- 1 tablespoon grated lemon zest
- 1/2 cup (1 stick) butter, softened
- 3 eggs

Streusel Topping

- 1/2 cup brown sugar
- 2 tablespoons all-purpose flour
- 2 tablespoons sugar
- 1/2 teaspoon cinnamon
- 1/2 cup chopped pecans
- 4 tablespoons butter, melted

TO MAKE THE BABKA, pour about 1/3 cup of the warm milk into a medium bowl, and sprinkle the yeast over it. Stir and press to dissolve the yeast, and then add the rest of the milk. Add the salt, 1 teaspoon of sugar, and 1 cup of flour. Beat to mix everything well, and then set aside on the counter to awaken the yeast, about 20 minutes.

MEANWHILE, generously butter a 10-inch tube or a Bundt pan. Combine the raisins and the lemon zest with the remaining 2 1/2 cups of flour. Toss to coat the raisins with flour and mix everything well.

COMBINE THE BUTTER and the remaining sugar in a large bowl. Beat well with a mixer at high speed, and then add the eggs and beat until soft, pale yellow, and fluffy. When the yeast mixture is thickened and puffy, add it to the egg and butter mixture, and beat at low speed just to combine everything well. You should have a thick but very soft dough. Cover with a kitchen towel and set aside in a warm spot to rise until the dough doubles in size, about 1 hour.

TO MAKE THE STREUSEL TOPPING, combine the brown sugar, flour, sugar, cinnamon, and pecans in a large bowl. Use your hands to mix everything well, rubbing it into a nice, crumbly streusel for your babka.

GIVE A FEW GOOD STIRS to deflate the dough, and then transfer it to the prepared tube pan. Drizzle the melted butter over the top of the cake, and then sprinkle the streusel topping all over its surface. Cover with a kitchen towel and set aside for about 45 minutes to rise for the final time.

TOWARD THE END of the babka's rising time, heat the oven to 375°F. After the babka has risen sufficiently, bake for 25 to 30 minutes, or until the cake is tall, fragrant, and nicely browned. Let the cake cool in the pan on a wire rack or folded kitchen towel for about 2 hours. Then loosen it carefully from the pan with a table knife, turn it out onto a wire rack, and place it top side up to cool completely.

This cake is the specialty of my stepmother, Virginia, and it tastes as wonderful as it looks. The icing is a scrumptious brown-sugar fudge, which needs to be spread onto the cooled cake quickly once it is ready. If it sets up too quickly while you are spreading it on the cake, return the pan to the stove and warm it gently over low heat, stirring in a spoonful or two of evaporated milk to make it creamy again. This will result in a harder icing, but it will still be delicious.

Gigi's Fabulous Caramel Cake

SERVES 8 TO 10

Yellow Cake

- 3/4 cup (1 1/2 sticks) butter
- 1 cup milk
- 2 cups sifted all-purpose flour
- 2 3/4 teaspoons baking powder
- 1/2 teaspoon salt
- 4 eggs
- 2 cups sugar
- 1 teaspoon vanilla extract

Gigi's Caramel Icing

- One 1-pound box (about 2 2/3 cups) light brown sugar
- 1/2 cup (1 stick) butter
- 7 tablespoons evaporated milk
- 1 teaspoon vanilla extract

TO MAKE THE CAKE, heat the oven to 325°F. Grease and flour two 9-inch round cake pans. Combine the butter and milk in a small saucepan, and cook over low heat until the butter melts. Stir well and let cool to room temperature.

MEANWHILE, combine the flour, baking powder, and salt in a medium bowl, and stir with a fork to mix well. In a large bowl, combine the eggs and sugar, and beat well at high speed, scraping down the bowl often, until light yellow, smooth, and thick.

STIR THE FLOUR MIXTURE into the egg mixture, mixing only until the flour disappears. Add the cooled milk mixture and the vanilla, stir well, and divide the batter between the prepared pans.

BAKE at 325°F for 25 to 30 minutes, until the cakes are a pale golden brown, spring back when touched lightly in the center, and begin to pull away from the sides of the pans.

COOL IN THE PANS for 10 minutes on wire racks or folded kitchen towels. Then turn out the cakes onto wire racks or plates to cool completely, top side up.

TO MAKE THE ICING, have the cake layers handy and ready for frosting, so that you can spread the warm frosting quickly once it is ready. In a heavy medium saucepan, combine the brown sugar, butter, evaporated milk, and vanilla. Bring to a boil over medium-high heat. Stir well and then adjust the heat so that the frosting boils and bubbles gently. Cook for 7 minutes. Remove from the heat and let cool for 5 minutes.

BEAT THE WARM ICING with a wooden spoon until it thickens, 2 to 3 minutes. Place a cake layer, top side down, on a cake stand or serving platter. Quickly spread some icing over the top, and cover it with the second cake layer, top side up. Ice the top quickly and then spread the remaining icing over the sides.

IF THE ICING BECOMES TOO HARD to spread, warm gently over low heat, add a spoonful or two of evaporated milk, and then scrape and stir well until the icing softens enough to spread again. Dip a table knife in very hot water to help soften and smooth out the icing once it is spread.

COCONUT CAKES

For many people, coconut cake is the ultimate Southern confection: fluffy and fancy, sweet and pretty, familiar, yet always capable of putting on a new outfit and making a big splash at the family reunion. My grandmother's coconut cake was the first one I ever encountered and remains my heart's delight. But even I have to admit that there is more than one way to make a fantastic coconut cake, and I adore baking the old-fashioned recipes and trying out the new ones.

Cracking open a fresh coconut for this kind of cake has its own ritual, bringing to mind a Christmas season kitchen scene, with Grandaddy sitting at the table helping out with the work of cracking, peeling, and grating a precious coconut for the season's grand event, Grandmother's coconut cake. My grandfather was seldom part of the kitchen team, but at Christmas he made oyster stew and helped my grandmother get the coconut all ready for her famous, glorious coconut cake.

That cake is here (page 62), along with my friend Robert Mullis's grandmother's cake (page 61). You'll also find a devastatingly delicious LEMON-FILLED COCONUT CAKE (page 65) that brings two contrasting flavors together in a magnificent way. COCONUT-CREAM CAKE (page 67) is simple to make because whipped cream is used as the frosting; I make that one when I feel like a quick assembly, with cracking the coconut being the only focused part of the cooking.

Don't let cracking open a coconut put you off making these cakes. You can buy frozen grated coconut at Asian markets, and you can also use shredded or flaked coconut, available in the baking supplies aisle, with lovely results. Its sweetness makes for a soft and luscious cake.

Many Southern cooks include coconut cake on the dessert table at Christmastime, alongside the eggnog, ambrosia, and fruitcake. You'll also see these cakes at garden parties, bake sales, and family reunions all year long. With coconut cake in your dessert repertoire, you will have a glorious centerpiece for the celebrations that are precious to you.

Fresh COCONUT 101

1 COCONUT YIELDS 3 TO 4½ CUPS OF GRATED COCONUT,
PLUS ½ TO 1 CUP OF CLEAR COCONUT JUICE

Choose a brown, hairy coconut that feels heavy and sounds like it's full of juice when you shake it. If possible, have someone help you, since this task calls for an abundance of hands-on work.

Set out a hammer and a large bowl or a 13-by-9-inch baking pan. If you are right-handed, hold the coconut in your left hand, directly over the bowl or pan, with the three "eyes" toward you and the peaked top pointed away from you. Imagine a little equator belting the coconut's circumference. To crack open the coconut, strike it with a bold hammer blow on that invisible equator line. Continue striking single, sharp, hard blows along the equator as you work your way around the coconut, rotating it in your palm after each blow. Continue until a deep sound and a gush of juice into the bowl signal that you have cracked a very tough nut.

BREAK OPEN THE COCONUT, using lighter blows as needed, letting the ½ to 1 cup of juice drain out into the bowl or pan. With a table knife, carefully pry the thick, white meat away from the thin, hard outer shell by inserting the knife blade between the two and twisting it to separate them. Break the coconut meat into smaller chunks, using either the hammer or your hands to continue separating the coconut meat from the shell.

STRAIN THE JUICE and set it aside to use in a cake batter or icing. Carefully peel away most of the thin, hard brown skin covering the exterior side of the coconut meat. You can use a very sturdy vegetable peeler, a paring knife, a chef's knife, or a cleaver. Give the peeled coconut pieces a good rinse, and you are ready to shred, slice, chop, grate, or grind them as needed.

TO GRIND THE COCONUT WITH A FOOD PROCESSOR, cut the peeled coconut meat into ½-inch chunks. Fit the food processor with the metal chopping blade and turn the machine on. Drop in the coconut chunks by the handful, and then stop to scrape down the sides. Process until you have a bowl full of coconut, finely chopped to an almost fluffy texture. You could also use a blender, working in batches, and stopping often to scrape the chopped meat and chunks away from the blades.

TO GRATE THE COCONUT WITH A BOX GRATER, leave the peeled pieces in large chunks. Grate them against the large holes or small ones, turning them often to protect your fingers. Gather the bits and end pieces of the coconut as you go, finely chop them by hand, and add them to the grated coconut. To use a hand-held rotary grater such as a Mouli, cut the coconut meat so the pieces will fit into the chamber, and grate them into a medium bowl.

This big, beautiful cake is the dowager empress of the royal family of coconut cakes. Layers of yellow cake are sandwiched together with sweet, fluffy white icing and finished with a blizzard of coconut shreds. The White Mountain Coconut Icing is based on **Classic Boiled Icing** (page 152), which is also known as divinity frosting. For an easier version, you can use **Seven-Minute Frosting** (page 147), which produces a similar icing with a bit less effort. If you crack open a fresh coconut for this cake (see page 57), include the juice as part of the liquid in the cake batter. For a little color and contrast, I like to spread a thin layer of raspberry or blackberry jam on the cake layers before icing them with the fluffy white frosting.

Classic Coconut Cake

SERVES 8 TO 10

Cake

- 3 cups all-purpose flour
- 2 teaspoons baking powder
- ½ teaspoon salt
- 1 teaspoon vanilla extract
- 1 cup milk, or juice from a fresh coconut plus enough milk added to make 1 cup
- 1 cup (2 sticks) butter, softened
- 2 cups sugar
- 4 eggs

White Mountain Coconut Icing

- 1 cup sugar
- ½ cup water
- 2 egg whites
- About 3 cups freshly grated coconut (see page 57), or sweetened shredded coconut

TO MAKE THE CAKE, heat the oven to 350°F. Grease and flour two 9-inch cake pans and set aside. In a medium bowl, combine the flour, baking powder, and salt, and use a fork to mix them together well. Stir the vanilla into the milk.

IN A LARGE BOWL, beat the softened butter with a mixer at medium speed until creamy. Add the sugar and continue beating, stopping to scrape down the sides, until the mixture is light and evenly combined. Add the eggs, one by one, beating well each time, until the mixture is thick and smooth.

ADD ABOUT ONE THIRD of the flour mixture to the batter and beat well at low speed. Then add about half the milk to the batter, beating well. Continue beating as you add another third of the flour mixture, followed by the rest of the milk, and then the remaining flour mixture, beating well each time until the batter is very thick and smooth.

QUICKLY SCRAPE THE BATTER into the prepared cake pans, dividing it evenly, and place them in the oven. Bake at 350°F for 25 to 30 minutes, until the cakes are golden brown, spring back when touched lightly in the center, and begin to pull away from the sides of the pans.

REMOVE FROM THE OVEN, and cool in the pans on wire racks or folded kitchen towels for 10 minutes. Then turn out the cakes onto wire racks or plates, turn the layers top side up, and cool completely. You could also split the layers horizontally to make 4 thin layers of cake.

TO MAKE THE ICING, stir the sugar into the water to dissolve it. Bring the mixture to a gentle boil, and cook without stirring for 3 minutes. Then boil for 5 to 10 minutes more, stirring often, until the syrup has thickened and will form itself into a thread about 2 inches long when poured from a spoon back into the pot. Set the syrup aside.

CONTINUED

CONTINUED

BEAT THE EGG WHITES in a large bowl with a mixer at high speed until they are bright white, shiny, and pillow up into voluminous clouds. While beating at high speed, slowly pour the cooked syrup into the egg whites to blend them together into a fluffy white icing, 4 to 5 minutes.

TO ICE THE CAKE, place one cake layer, top side down, on a cake stand or serving plate. Cover it generously with icing and sprinkle with coconut. Place the second layer on top of the iced layer, top side up. First ice the sides to help keep the cake steady, and then spread icing generously over the top, completely covering the cake. Place the cake stand or serving plate on a cookie sheet to catch any loose coconut as you shower the cake. Sprinkle coconut all over the cake, and then gently pat handfuls of coconut onto the sides and top to cover any bare spots. Transfer any leftover coconut to a jar or resealable plastic bag and store it in the freezer.

Like me, my friend Robert Mullis remembers his grandfather lending a rare hand in the kitchen each Christmas, when his grandmother, Pearl Mae Oakley, set about making her famous coconut cake. He did the grating, and she did the rest, creating a simple, lovely cake with delicate drizzles of icing drifting lazily down its sides. The completed cake was moved to a screened-in porch for a day, so it could set up and mellow without tempting family members to sample the holiday centerpiece ahead of time. Robert's grandmother knew her recipe was a winner—she advised visitors, "You just eat that with coffee and you'll love it!"

Pearl Mae Oakley's Coconut Cake

SERVES 8 TO 10

Pearl Mae's Yellow Cake

- 3 cups all-purpose flour
- 2 teaspoons baking powder
- ½ teaspoon salt
- 1 teaspoon vanilla extract
- 1 cup milk
- 1 cup (2 sticks) butter, softened
- 2 cups sugar
- 4 eggs

Pearl Mae's Coconut Icing

- 2 cups sugar (or 1 cup if you are using sweetened shredded coconut)
- 1 cup milk
- Butter the size of an egg (¼ cup)
- About 3 cups grated fresh coconut (see page 57), or sweetened shredded coconut

TO MAKE THE CAKE, heat the oven to 350°F. Grease and flour two 9-inch round cake pans and set aside. In a medium bowl, combine the flour, baking powder, and salt, and use a fork to mix them together well. Stir the vanilla into the milk.

IN A LARGE BOWL, beat the softened butter with a mixer at high speed until creamy. Add the sugar gradually, stopping to scrape down the bowl, and continue beating until the mixture is evenly combined. Add the eggs, one by one, beating well each time, until the mixture is thick and smooth.

ADD ABOUT ONE THIRD of the flour mixture to the batter and beat well with the mixer at medium speed. Then add about half the milk to the batter, beating well. Continue beating as you add another third of the flour mixture, the remaining milk, and then the remaining flour mixture. Beat well until very thick and smooth.

QUICKLY SCRAPE THE BATTER into the prepared cake pans, dividing it evenly, and place them in the oven. Bake at 350°F for 25 to 30 minutes, until the cakes are golden, spring back when touched lightly in the center, and begin to pull away from the sides of the pans.

REMOVE FROM THE OVEN, and cool the layers in the pans on wire racks or folded kitchen towels for 10 minutes. Then turn out the cakes onto wire racks or plates, top side up, and cool completely.

TO MAKE THE ICING, combine the sugar, milk, and butter in a medium saucepan, and cook over medium heat, stirring now and then, until the sugar dissolves and everything melts into a smooth, velvety icing, 3 to 4 minutes. Stir in the grated coconut and set aside.

TO COMPLETE THE CAKE, place one layer, top side down, on a serving plate, and spoon about half the icing over the cake. Place the second layer over the first, top side up, and spoon the remaining icing over its surface. Work slowly, allowing the icing to soak into the cake a bit. Continue spooning icing over the cake, allowing it to run down the sides as it will. Let stand for about 1 hour before cutting.

This is the cake that made my grandmother famous all over Orange and Durham Counties, in the Piedmont region of North Carolina, during my childhood. Fresh coconut is ideal here, and worth every bit of the effort it requires. But use sweetened shredded coconut, available in the baking aisles of most supermarkets, or frozen grated coconut from an Asian market, if that helps you get the cake made. My grandmother usually baked this cake in two 9-inch layers and then split them horizontally to make 4 thin layers. It is also lovely baked in three 8-inch layers.

Miss Nannie's Fresh Coconut Cake

SERVES 8 TO 10

TO MAKE THE CAKE, heat the oven to 350°F. Grease and flour two 9-inch round cake pans and set aside. In a large bowl, beat the softened butter with a mixer at medium speed until creamy. Add the sugar and continue beating, stopping to scrape down the bowl, until the mixture is fluffy and fairly smooth. Add the eggs, one by one, beating each time, until you have a thick, smooth batter.

IN A MEDIUM BOWL, combine the flour, baking powder, and salt, and use a fork to mix them together well. Stir the vanilla into the milk.

ADD ABOUT ONE THIRD of the flour mixture to the batter and beat with a mixer at low speed just until the flour disappears. Add about half the milk to the batter, beating just until the batter is smooth. Continue beating as you add another third of the flour mixture to the batter, followed by the rest of the milk, and then the remaining flour mixture, beating each time just until the batter is very thick and smooth.

QUICKLY SCRAPE THE BATTER into the prepared cake pans, dividing it evenly, and place them in the oven. Bake at 350°F for 25 to 30 minutes, until the cakes are golden, spring back lightly when touched in the center, and begin to pull away from the sides of the pans. Remove from the oven and cool the cakes in the pans on wire racks or folded kitchen towels for 10 minutes. Then turn out the cakes onto wire racks or plates. Turn the layers top side up to cool completely. Just before icing the cake, carefully slice each layer in half horizontally to make 4 thin layers.

TO MAKE THE ICING, combine the sugar and flour in a heavy medium saucepan, and stir with a fork to mix them together well. Stir in the coconut milk, and place over medium

Miss Nannie's Cake

- 1 cup (2 sticks) butter, softened
- 2 cups sugar
- 4 eggs
- 3 cups all-purpose flour
- 2 teaspoons baking powder
- ½ teaspoon salt
- 2 teaspoons vanilla extract
- 1 cup milk

Miss Nannie's Fresh Coconut Icing

- 3 cups sugar
- 3 rounded tablespoons flour or cornstarch
- 1 cup fresh coconut milk, or water, or a combination of the two
- About 3 cups freshly grated coconut (see page 57), or sweetened shredded coconut

heat. Cook, stirring often, until the mixture comes to a gentle boil. Continue to stir often as the sugar dissolves and the mixture turns syrupy. Cook for about 4 minutes at a gentle boil, and then stir in about 2¼ cups of the freshly grated coconut. Cook for about 2 minutes more, stirring gently as the icing thickens. Remove from the heat and let cool to room temperature.

TO ICE THE CAKE, place one thin layer, top side down, on a cake stand or serving plate, and spread about one fourth of the icing over the cake. Repeat with the remaining 3 layers, placing the fourth layer top side up. Spread the icing over the top to the edges and let it cascade gently down the sides. Sprinkle the remaining ¾ cup of coconut over the top of the cake, and pat gently to help it adhere to the icing.

THE CAKE WILL BE VISIBLE through the translucent icing, looking as though it were in a little ice palace. Let the cake stand at room temperature for 2 to 3 hours, or as long as overnight. Cover the cake well and store it in the refrigerator if you will not be serving it within a few hours. Simply let the cake return to room temperature for 1 or 2 hours to release the strong chill before serving. This cake mellows and tastes even better the second day.

Coconut cake is always very sweet, and luscious lemon curd provides a sunburst of tangy flavor that I adore. You can buy it at specialty food shops, but lemon curd is also simple to make. Once you know how, you can share small jars as gifts for your most precious friends, or enjoy it on breakfast biscuits or teatime scones. Whether you make the lemon curd yourself or buy it, you can skip the frosting by covering the cake layers with whipped cream and showering the cake with coconut flakes, as in **Coconut Cream Cake** (page 67). Berry jam makes a marvelous filling for coconut cake as well. You can split the layers to make four thin layers and double the lemon curd or jam for a sublime version of this cake.

Lemon-Filled Coconut Cake

SERVES 8 TO 10

Cake

- 2½ cups self-rising flour (see Note, page 66)
- 1½ cups sugar
- 1 teaspoon vanilla extract
- 1 cup milk
- ½ cup (1 stick) butter, softened, or ½ cup shortening
- 3 eggs

Fluffy White Frosting

- 1 cup sugar
- ¼ cup light corn syrup
- ¼ cup water
- 2 egg whites
- ¼ teaspoon cream of tartar
- ¼ teaspoon salt
- 1 teaspoon vanilla extract
- 1 recipe **Lemon Curd** (page 157), or 1 cup store-bought lemon curd or blackberry or raspberry jam
- About 3 cups freshly grated coconut (see page 57), or sweetened shredded coconut

TO MAKE THE CAKE, heat the oven to 350°F, and grease and flour two 9-inch round cake pans. Combine the flour and sugar in a large bowl, and mix with a fork to blend them well. Stir the vanilla into the milk.

ADD the butter, eggs, and ¼ cup of the milk to the flour mixture. Blend well with a mixer at medium speed, stopping now and then to scrape down the bowl, until you have a thick, fairly smooth batter, about 2 minutes. Add the remaining ¾ cup milk, and beat only until the batter is smooth and well combined.

SCRAPE THE BATTER into the prepared pans and bake at 350°F for 25 to 30 minutes, until the cakes are golden brown, spring back when touched lightly at the center, and begin to pull away from the sides of the pans.

COOL THE CAKES in the pans on wire racks or folded kitchen towels for 10 minutes. Carefully turn them out onto the wire racks or onto plates, top side up, and cool completely.

TO MAKE THE FROSTING, bring about 3 inches of water to a boil in a medium saucepan or in the bottom of a double boiler. Meanwhile, combine the sugar, corn syrup, water, egg whites, cream of tartar, and salt in a large, heat-proof bowl that will fit snugly over the saucepan, or in the top of the double boiler. Beat for 1 minute with a mixer at low speed, until the egg white mixture is pale yellow, foamy, and well combined.

PLACE THE MIXING BOWL or the double boiler top over the pan of boiling water, and adjust the heat to maintain a gentle boil. Using a hand-held electric mixer, beat the sugar–egg white mixture at high speed for 7 to 14 minutes, or until it triples in volume, swelling into a voluptuous cloud of frosting that holds firm, curly peaks when the beaters are lifted. Remove from the heat, add the vanilla, and beat for 2 minutes more, scraping down the bowl once or twice.

CONTINUED

CONTINUED

TO ASSEMBLE THE CAKE, place one layer, top side down, on a cake stand or serving plate. Cover it generously with the lemon curd, spreading it almost to the edge of the cake. Place the other layer, top side up, on top of the lemon curd. Cover the cake generously with the frosting, and then place it on a cookie sheet or tray to catch any coconut that doesn't stick to the cake. Sprinkle coconut generously all over the iced layers, and then carefully pat coconut on any bare spots.

NOTE: If you don't have self-rising flour, combine 2½ cups of all-purpose flour, 2½ teaspoons of baking powder, 1¼ teaspoons salt, and a rounded ½ teaspoon (about ⅝ teaspoon) of baking soda.

Lovely, simple, cool, and fresh, this is a coconut cake that would even hit the spot on a hot summer day. Prepare it ahead, making the cake layers and grating or setting out the coconut. Then you can whip up the cream and quickly assemble the cake when you are ready to produce a spectacular, but not exhausting, dessert. You could also create a little inner beauty by icing each layer with strawberry, raspberry, or blackberry jam before spreading on the whipped-cream frosting.

Coconut-Cream Cake

SERVES 8 TO 10

Cake

- 2 cups sifted all-purpose flour
- 1¼ cups sugar
- 2 teaspoons baking powder
- ½ teaspoon salt
- 3 eggs
- 1 teaspoon vanilla extract
- 1¼ cups heavy cream or whipping cream

Coconut-Cream Frosting

- 1½ cups cold heavy cream or whipping cream
- 3 tablespoons confectioners' sugar
- About 3 cups coconut, either freshly grated (see page 57) or sweetened shredded coconut

TO MAKE THE CAKE, heat the oven to 350°F. Grease two 9-inch cake pans, line the bottoms with waxed paper or kitchen parchment, and then dust with flour. In a medium bowl, combine the flour, sugar, baking powder, and salt. Stir with a fork to mix well. In a small bowl, combine the eggs and vanilla, and beat well with a fork until frothy.

IN A LARGE BOWL, beat the cream with a mixer at high speed until it thickens and swells to form stiff peaks, 2 to 3 minutes. Add the egg-vanilla mixture and beat at medium speed until just blended. Add the flour mixture and use a spatula or a large spoon to fold it in gently, just until the flour disappears.

QUICKLY TRANSFER THE BATTER to the prepared pans, and bake at 350°F for 20 to 25 minutes, until the layers are golden, spring back when touched lightly in the center, and begin to pull away from the sides of the pans. Cool in the pans on wire racks or folded kitchen towels for 10 minutes. Then turn out the cakes onto wire racks and cool completely, top side up.

TO MAKE THE FROSTING, in a large bowl, beat the cream with a mixer at high speed until it swells into thick clouds and holds a soft peak when you lift up the beaters. Sprinkle on the confectioners' sugar, and continue beating, scraping the bowl often, until the cream is thick and very firm, but still velvety smooth, 3 to 5 minutes. Ice the cake at once, or cover the bowl and chill it until it's time to complete the cake.

TO COMPLETE THE CAKE, place one layer top side down on a cake stand or serving plate, and put the cake stand on a cookie sheet or tray to catch any coconut that doesn't stick to the cake. Cover the cake layer generously with about one third of the cream. Sprinkle about one third of the grated coconut over it, and place the second layer on top. Ice the sides, then the top of the cake. Press the remaining coconut gently onto the whipped cream. Refrigerate until shortly before serving time.

Pineapple sings out a sweet-sharp summery note when included in the rich confection that is coconut cake. Making the simple filling is quick work, and you can compose the cake using any layers and frosting that you like best. This version combines a simple yellow layer cake and an ethereal, meringuelike icing topped with a blizzard of coconut. Try it with **Everyday Confectioners' Sugar Frosting** (page 146), replacing the milk with spoonfuls of pineapple juice; or use **Cream Cheese Frosting** (page 148) for a tangy counterpoint to the sweet components of the cake. Make the pineapple filling while the cake is baking, and whip up the glossy white frosting when the cake is cool enough to be iced.

Pineapple-Coconut Cake

SERVES 6 TO 8

Yellow Cake

- 3/4 cup (1 1/2 sticks) butter
- 1 cup milk
- 2 cups all-purpose flour
- 2 3/4 teaspoons baking powder
- 1/2 teaspoon salt
- 4 eggs
- 2 cups sugar
- 1 teaspoon vanilla extract

Pineapple Filling

- One 20-ounce can crushed pineapple (do not drain)
- 2/3 cup sugar
- 3 tablespoons butter
- 3 tablespoons all-purpose flour
- Generous pinch of salt

TO MAKE THE CAKE, heat the oven to 325°F and grease and flour two 9-inch or three 8-inch round cake pans. Combine the butter and milk in a small saucepan, and cook over low heat until the butter melts. Stir well and set aside to cool to room temperature.

MEANWHILE, in a medium bowl, stir together the flour, baking powder, and salt with a fork, and set aside. In a large bowl combine the eggs and sugar, and beat well at high speed, scraping down the bowl often, until the mixture is pale yellow, smooth, and thick.

STIR THE FLOUR MIXTURE into the egg mixture, using a large spoon or spatula to mix only until the flour disappears. Add the cooled milk and the vanilla, stir until smooth, and divide the batter between the prepared cake pans.

BAKE at 325°F for 25 to 30 minutes, until the cakes are golden, spring back when touched lightly at the center, and begin to pull away from the sides of the pans. Cool in the pans on wire racks or folded kitchen towels for 10 minutes. Then turn out the cakes onto wire racks or plates to cool completely, top side up.

TO MAKE THE FILLING, in a medium saucepan, combine the pineapple, sugar, butter, flour, and salt, and bring to a gentle boil over medium-high heat. Reduce the heat to maintain a gentle simmer, and cook for about 5 minutes, stirring often, until the butter melts and everything comes together into a chunky sauce. Remove from the heat and cool to room temperature.

Fluffy Pineapple Frosting

- 2 egg whites
- 1½ cups sugar
- ⅓ cup pineapple juice
- 1 tablespoon light corn syrup
- 2 cups sweetened shredded coconut

TO MAKE THE FROSTING, bring about 3 inches of water to an active simmer in the bottom of a double boiler or a medium saucepan. In the top of the double boiler, or in a heat-proof bowl that will sit snugly over the saucepan, combine the egg whites, sugar, pineapple juice, and corn syrup. Beat with an electric mixer at medium speed for 1 minute, until the mixture is pale yellow and very foamy. Place the double boiler top or the bowl over the simmering water, increase the speed to medium-high, and beat for 7 minutes or more, until the icing becomes white, thick, and shiny, and triples in volume. Continue beating until the frosting forms soft peaks. (This process could take as long as 15 minutes.) Remove the frosting from the heat and beat for 2 minutes more. Frost the cakes as soon as possible.

TO COMPLETE THE CAKE, place one cake layer, top side down, on a cake stand or serving plate, and cover it with about half of the Pineapple Filling. Spread the filling almost to the edge of the cake. Place the other layer, top side up, on the filling, and spread it with the remaining filling. Cover the sides and then the top of the cake generously with the frosting. Place the cake on a cookie sheet or tray to catch any coconut that doesn't stick to the cake. Sprinkle the shredded coconut generously all over the top and sides of the cake, and then carefully pat coconut on any bare spots.

In her writing, Eudora Welty often uses food to illuminate her stories of Southern life, and nowhere more deliciously than in her novel *Delta Wedding*. Welty scholar Dr. Ann Romines, a professor of English at George Washington University, explores this aspect of Welty's work in two fine essays, "Reading the Cakes: 'Delta Wedding' and the Texts of Southern Women's Culture" and "Baking the Cake: My Recipe for Mashula's Coconut Cake." Working from the general references within *Delta Wedding*, Dr. Romines created this recipe, which makes a spectacular cake. Look for almond paste in baking aisles, or order from The Baker's Catalogue (page 161).

Mashula's Coconut Cake

SERVES 6 TO 8

TO MAKE THE CAKE, heat the oven to 350°F, and grease three or four 8-inch round cake pans. Line each pan with a circle of waxed paper or kitchen parchment, and grease the waxed paper. Combine the flour, baking powder, salt, and nutmeg in a medium bowl, and stir with a fork to mix everything well.

IN A LARGE BOWL, cream together the butter and 1 cup of the sugar with a mixer at high speed, beating until light and well-combined. Beat in the extracts and lemon zest.

IN A MEDIUM BOWL, beat the egg whites until foamy. Gradually beat in the remaining ½ cup of sugar, 1 tablespoon at a time, until soft peaks form. (An electric mixer is especially useful here, but of course it can be done by hand, as Mashula did!)

ADD ABOUT ONE THIRD of the flour mixture to the batter and beat well with a mixer at medium speed. Then add about half the milk to the batter, beating well. Continue beating as you add another third of the flour mixture, followed by the rest of the milk, and then the remaining flour mixture. Beat until smooth, but do not overmix.

GENTLY FOLD IN about half the beaten egg whites with a wooden spoon or a rubber spatula. Fold in the remaining egg whites. Divide the batter among the prepared pans. Run a knife through the batter in each pan to break up any air bubbles, and rap each pan sharply on a flat surface about 5 times to distribute the batter evenly.

ARRANGE THE PANS in the oven with at least 1 inch between them. If you are baking 4 layers, you may need to bake them 2 at a time, as Ellen did in *Delta Wedding*. Bake at 350°F until the layers are lightly browned and begin to pull away from the sides of the pans, and the center of each layer springs back when touched lightly. This will take between 15 and 25 minutes, depending on the thickness of your layers. To keep your cakes tender, do not overbake.

Cake

- 2¾ cups sifted cake flour
- 1 tablespoon baking powder
- ½ teaspoon salt
- ¼ teaspoon ground nutmeg
- ¾ cup (1½ sticks) butter, softened
- 1½ cups sugar
- 1 teaspoon vanilla extract
- ½ teaspoon almond extract (optional)
- 1 teaspoon grated lemon zest
- ¾ cup egg whites (about 6 large eggs, or 12 to 14 guinea eggs)
- 1 cup milk

Almond Filling

- ½ cup sugar
- ¼ teaspoon salt
- ¼ cup cornstarch
- 2 cups milk
- 4 egg yolks (or 8 to 10 guinea egg yolks), lightly beaten
- 4 ounces almond paste or marzipan
- 1 teaspoon vanilla extract
- ½ teaspoon almond extract

Frosting

- ½ cup (1 stick) butter, softened
- 1½ teaspoons vanilla extract
- ½ teaspoon almond extract
- 1 teaspoon brandy (optional)
- ⅛ teaspoon salt
- One 1-pound box (about 3⅔ cups) confectioners' sugar
- 2 or 3 tablespoons whipping cream, half-and-half, or milk
- 2 cups grated fresh coconut (see page 57), or sweetened shredded or flaked coconut
- 24 perfect almond halves

COOL IN THE PANS on wire racks or folded kitchen towels for 10 minutes. Then carefully turn out the cakes on wire racks or plates. Remove the papers (enjoy the "golden scrapement") and turn, top side up, to cool completely. Assemble the cake as soon as the layers are cool.

TO MAKE THE FILLING, in a heavy medium saucepan, combine the sugar, salt, and cornstarch. Whisk in the milk, working very slowly at first to avoid lumps. Bring the mixture to a boil over medium-high heat, stirring often, and then boil for 1 minute, or until the mixture begins to thicken. Remove from the heat. Add about ⅓ cup of the hot milk mixture to the egg yolks, and stir to blend them quickly and well. Pour the warmed egg yolk mixture into the saucepan, stirring hard to combine it with the milk mixture quickly and well. Then place about 1 cup of the mixture in a medium bowl, and work in the almond paste, stirring, scraping, pressing, and mashing with a fork until fairly smooth, 3 to 4 minutes. Scrape this almond paste mixture into the pan and bring it back to a boil, stirring often. Boil for 1 minute, or until thickened. Remove from the heat and add the extracts. Let the filling cool slightly, then cover and refrigerate until completely cool.

TO MAKE THE FROSTING, in a large bowl, combine the butter, vanilla, almond extract, brandy, if using, and salt. Mix well by hand or with an electric mixer. Then beat in the confectioners' sugar, cautiously adding just enough cream or milk to make a spreadable mixture.

TO COMPLETE THE CAKE, put the thickest layer, top side down, on a cake stand or serving plate. Spread it with filling. Don't take the filling quite to the edges of the layer, or it will ooze out. If the filling seems too thick to spread, thin it with a little milk. But it should be fairly thick. Repeat with layers, except for the final one. Place the last layer, which should be your thinnest, top side up.

ICE THE CAKE with the prepared frosting, covering the sides first, and then piling all the remaining frosting "thick on the top," as Ellen does. Then cover the entire cake with the grated coconut, pressing lightly to make it adhere. Let the cake firm up for a few minutes, and then decorate with the 24 almond halves, placing them "close enough to touch." In *Delta Wedding* style, present the cake on a footed glass cake stand, and serve it on your best small china plates, like "those little Dabney plates" that Ellen uses.

FRUITCAKES AND OTHER HOLIDAY FAVORITES

I know all the fruitcake jokes: the doorstop joke, the sneaking-it-to-an-unsuspecting-family-member-during-the-annual-gift-exchange joke, and the theory that there is really only one fruitcake out there, circulating continually throughout the world. Proponents of that last theory were obviously not with me on a recent bus tour of a fruitcake factory in Corsicana, Texas, nor have they seen the huge annual fruitcake display at my local grocery store.

Although I adore fruitcake in almost all its forms, those jokes do not hurt my feelings, nor do they even make me mad. First of all, we need all the jokes and laughter we can come up with in this sweet old world, and secondly, liking fruitcake is not a required life skill. Truth is, if it debuted as a new product this coming Christmas, it would never survive, much less endure, because it does not fit with contemporary lifestyles and tastes.

Fruitcake achieved mythic status over time, and is a direct descendant of European medieval sweets made with honey and dried fruit, and, later, the boiled and steamed puddings of Victorian England. In this country, fruitcake was preceded in the Colonial era by great cakes, black cakes, and Dundee cakes. Dark and light fruitcakes followed, and there were a host of other varieties, some of which have mercifully been retired from the kitchen. But fruitcakes survive, and I, for one, am glad.

When Bob Cratchit comes home with that teeny-tiny Christmas pudding, those children whoop as though Grammaw had brought them a puppy and a pony during the same visit. It isn't the pudding itself, which is meant to be seen as quite modest in contrast to its reception *chez* Cratchit. It's the symbol of plenty, the cue for the music to begin and the lights to go down on a memory or a wish or both. It's the birthday cake in a darkened room with candles blazing, the national anthem at a minor-league baseball game, the first scent of coffee brewing when your partner gets up before you do. Fruitcake historically came riding into our culture on the winter holiday train, and that still has power, even if some of us would really rather have cheesecake, brownies, or tiramisu.

I say long live fruitcake, because I like to eat it and to bake it, too. But if you don't, keep the book open. This chapter starts with fruitcake, but soon runs off down the road to all manner of other parties. From the Blue Ridge Mountains, there is ORANGE SLICE CAKE WITH ORANGE GLAZE (page 78); and then there is my MOTHER'S CINNAMON-PECAN COFFEE CAKE (page 87), a celebration breakfast for Christmas or any old time of year. My friend John Whitener shares his version of the luscious TRES LECHES CAKE (page 85), easy, elegant, and portable for times when you need to arrive at the party with the cake.

For the Jewish New Year there's SISTER SADIE'S ROSH HASHANAH HONEY CAKE (page 91), and for Passover try the dynamite meringue cake, MAW MAW'S SLIP AND SLIDE PASSOVER TORTE (page 90), filled with fresh sweet berries and topped with a cloud of whipped cream. The theme is celebration and tradition, but not just any old tradition. Let this collection get you thinking about your past and present, and start you baking special cakes every holiday season, to share with those who are precious to you.

Dark fruitcakes take their deep brown hue from the intensely colored and flavored ingredients enriching their batter. First comes molasses, sorghum, or cane syrup, followed by a bouquet of spices, including cinnamon, nutmeg, cloves, allspice, and mace. Stir in a generous scoop of last summer's home-canned blackberry jam or fig preserves, or store-bought jam or jelly, and finish up with a good dose of spirits: a wineglass full of brandy, bourbon, sherry, or dark rum. Traditional ingredients can draw out a fruitcake recipe's ingredients list to a daunting length. I've listed total amounts for candied and dried fruits, so that you can fill your dark fruitcake with your particular favorites.

Classic Dark Fruitcake

SERVES 15 TO 20

HEAT THE OVEN to 250°F. Generously grease a 10-inch tube pan or two 9-by-5-inch loaf pans. Line the bottom with waxed paper or kitchen parchment, grease the paper, and dust the pan and paper with flour.

COMBINE the flour, baking powder, salt, and spices in a medium bowl and stir with a fork to mix well. Combine the chopped pecans, walnuts, and dried and candied fruit in a large bowl, and add about ½ cup of the flour mixture. Use your hands to toss the fruit and nuts well to break up any sticky clusters and coat every piece with a little flour.

IN A LARGE BOWL, combine the butter and the sugar. Beat with a mixer at high speed for 2 to 3 minutes, stopping once or twice to scrape down the bowl, until the mixture is fluffy and well combined. Add the eggs, one by one, beating well and scraping the bowl after each one. The batter should be soft and thick. Add the jam, molasses, and orange zest, and beat just until you have a smooth, rich brown batter.

ADD half of the remaining flour mixture and half the orange juice, beating or stirring with a wooden spoon after each addition only until the flour or juice disappears into the batter. Repeat with the remaining flour and juice. Add the fruits and nuts, and stir to mix everything evenly and well. The batter will be thick and stiff.

SCOOP OR SCRAPE THE BATTER into the prepared pan, and bake at 250°F for 2½ to 3 hours, until the cake springs back when touched gently in the center, is pulling away from the sides of the pan, and a long wooden skewer inserted into the center comes out clean. (If you baked the cake in loaf pans, check them a few minutes early.)

1½ cups all-purpose flour

½ teaspoon baking powder

¼ teaspoon salt

1 teaspoon ground cinnamon

½ teaspoon ground nutmeg

¼ teaspoon ground cloves

¼ teaspoon ground allspice

2 cups coarsely chopped pecans

1½ cups coarsely chopped walnuts

7 cups total of candied and dried fruit of your choice, chopped into small chunks (candied cherries and pineapple, dried apricots, dates, currants, and raisins are some to consider)

½ cup (1 stick) butter, softened

1 cup dark brown sugar

3 eggs

⅓ cup jam or preserves, such as blackberry, fig, or strawberry

⅓ cup molasses or sorghum

1 tablespoon grated orange zest

½ cup orange juice

COOL THE CAKE in the pan on a wire rack or folded kitchen towel for 30 minutes. Loosen the cake from the sides of the pan with a table knife. Carefully remove the cake from the pan, peel off the paper, and set it, right side up, on a wire rack to cool completely.

TO STORE THE CAKE, wrap it tightly in foil, and store in a cake tin at room temperature for up to 2 weeks. If you like, season it every 4 to 5 days with a generous sprinkling of spirits, such as sherry, bourbon, whiskey, or rum.

Eudora Welty's White Fruitcake

Eudora Welty's stories and novels resonate with the rhythms of the kitchen and the roles that food and cooking play in women's lives. Miss Welty was a fine cook who enjoyed sharing recipes. In December 1980, she and one of her publishers, Albondocani Press, sent out a handsome holiday greeting card, which included this recipe. Miss Welty's family kindly gave permission for me to include it here. This recipe is reproduced here exactly as she wrote it, including the use of the abbreviation "tsp." in place of "teaspoon." Regarding the options Miss Welty offers, I use 1 teaspoon of grated lemon zest and ½ teaspoon of nutmeg, and I don't use any citron. I love red crystallized cherries so much that I use all red ones and no green ones.

1½ cups butter

2 cups sugar

6 eggs, separated

4 cups flour,
sifted before measuring

flour for fruit and nuts

2 tsp. baking powder

pinch of salt

1 pound pecan meats
(halves, preferably)

1 pound crystallized cherries,
half green, half red

1 pound crystallized pineapple, clear

some citron or lemon peel
if desired

1 cup bourbon

1 tsp. vanilla

nutmeg if desired

MAKE THE CAKE several weeks ahead of Christmas if you can.

THE RECIPE makes three medium-sized cakes or one large and one small. Prepare the pans—the sort with a chimney or tube—by greasing them well with Crisco and then lining them carefully with three layers of waxed paper, all greased as well.

PREPARE THE FRUIT AND NUTS AHEAD. Cut the pineapple in thin slivers and the cherries in half. Break up the pecan meats, reserving a handful or so shapely halves to decorate the tops of the cakes. Put in separate bowls, dusting fruit and nuts lightly in siftings of flour, to keep them from clustering together in the batter.

IN A VERY LARGE WIDE MIXING BOWL (a salad bowl or even a dishpan will serve) cream the butter very light, then beat in the sugar until all is smooth and creamy. Sift in the flour, with baking powder and salt added, a little at a time, alternating with the unbeaten egg yolks added one at a time. When all this is creamy, add the floured fruits and nuts gradually, scattering them lightly into the batter, stirring all the while, and add the bourbon in alternation, little by little. Lastly, whip the egg whites into peaks and fold in.

SET THE OVEN LOW, about 250. Pour the batter into the cake-pans, remembering that they will rise. Decorate the tops with nuts. Bake for three hours or more, until they spring back to the touch and a straw inserted at the center comes out clean and dry. (If the top browns too soon, lay a sheet of foil lightly over.) When done, the cakes should be a warm golden color.

WHEN THEY'VE COOLED ENOUGH to handle, run a spatula around the sides of each cake, cover the pan with a big plate, turn the pan over and slip the cake out. Cover the cake with another plate and turn it right side up. When cool, the cake can be wrapped in cloth or foil and stored in a tightly fitting tin box.

FROM TIME TO TIME before Christmas you may improve it with a little more bourbon, dribbled over the top to be absorbed and so ripen the cake before cutting. This cake will keep for a good while, in or out of the refrigerator.

—*Eudora Welty*

Also known as sugar plum cake, this sweet holiday fruitcake goes back more than four generations, to a time when even one fresh orange was a precious Christmas treat in many Southern homes. Beloved throughout my home state of North Carolina, it is also cherished in the Blue Ridge and Great Smoky Mountain regions of Kentucky, West Virginia, Virginia, North Carolina, Tennessee, and Georgia.

Orange Slice Cake *with Orange Glaze*

SERVES 6 TO 8

You can find orange slice candy in cellophane sacks among the candy in drugstores and grocery stores. Use a lightly buttered or oiled knife or kitchen scissors to chop the candy and dates into small pieces. Plan on pouring the simple orange glaze over the cake while it is still hot from the oven. Freshly squeezed orange juice and grated orange zest are wonderful in the glaze, but everyday orange juice sans orange zest will still provide a fine finish for your cake.

Cake

- 3¾ cups all-purpose flour
- ½ teaspoon salt
- 1 pound orange slice candy, chopped (about 3 cups)
- 2 cups chopped pecans or walnuts
- One 8-ounce package dates, chopped (about 1½ cups)
- 1 cup sweetened shredded coconut
- 1 cup (2 sticks) butter, softened
- 2 cups sugar
- 4 eggs
- 1 teaspoon baking soda
- ½ cup buttermilk (see Note)

TO MAKE THE CAKE, heat the oven to 300°F. Generously grease a 10-inch tube pan, line the bottom with waxed paper or kitchen parchment, and grease the paper. Combine the flour and salt in a small bowl, and put the orange slice candy, pecans, dates, and coconut in a large bowl. Sprinkle about one third of the flour over the candied fruit-and-nut mixture, and toss to separate the sticky pieces and coat everything evenly with the flour.

IN A VERY LARGE BOWL, combine the butter and sugar and beat with a mixer at high speed until light and fluffy. Beat in the eggs, one at a time, beating well each time and scraping down the bowl now and then, until you once again have a light, fluffy mixture. Stir in half the remaining flour, beating on low speed only until it disappears. Stir the soda into the buttermilk, add half of it to the batter, and stir well. Stir in the remaining flour, and then the buttermilk, mixing after each addition only until the batter is smooth. Add the orange slice mixture, flour and all, and mix well. Use a wooden spoon or your hands to combine everything into a thick, heavy, well-mixed batter.

CONTINUED

CONTINUED

SCOOP THE BATTER into the prepared pan and smooth the top of the cake. Bake at 300°F for 1½ to 2 hours, until the cake is golden brown, pulling away from the sides of the pan, and a wooden skewer inserted in the center comes out clean.

WHILE THE CAKE IS BAKING, make the glaze. Combine the sugar, orange juice, and zest in a medium bowl and stir well with a fork or a wooden spoon, until you have a smooth glaze.

WHEN THE CAKE IS DONE, place it in its pan, on a wire rack or a folded kitchen towel, and pour the Orange Glaze over the hot cake. Leave the cake in the pan to cool completely.

TO SERVE, carefully loosen the cooled, glazed cake from the pan with a table knife or rubber spatula. Gently turn the cake out of the pan onto a plate, remove the paper, and place it top side up on a cake stand or serving plate.

NOTE: If you don't have buttermilk, stir 1½ teaspoons of vinegar or lemon juice into ½ cup of milk, and let stand for 10 minutes.

Fresh Orange Glaze

2 cups confectioners' sugar

1 cup orange juice, freshly squeezed if possible

1 tablespoon grated orange zest (optional)

Why this sweet holiday celebration cake should bear this curious and confusing name is a mystery. Nothing about it is remotely Japanese, nor does it qualify as a fruitcake in any traditionally Southern definition of the word. Like classic fruitcake, it is enjoyed widely throughout the South as a holiday-season celebration cake. It contains raisins, spices, lemon and orange zest, and fresh coconut, so let's all welcome it to the fruitcake family with a big ol' hug. Think of it as a luscious layer cake containing spices, pecans, and raisins in two of its four layers. A coconut-orange glaze adorns the surface of the cake in a lacy, citrus-kissed curtain, tempting you to ask for a big slice of it, no matter what it is called.

Japanese Fruitcake

SERVES 8 TO 10

Cake

- 3 cups all-purpose flour
- 2 teaspoons baking powder
- ½ teaspoon salt
- 1 cup chopped raisins or whole currants
- 1 cup chopped pecans or walnuts
- 1½ teaspoons ground cinnamon
- 1½ teaspoons ground allspice
- ½ teaspoon ground cloves
- 1 cup (2 sticks) butter, softened
- 2 cups sugar
- 4 eggs
- 1 teaspoon vanilla extract
- 1 cup milk

TO MAKE THE CAKE, heat the oven to 350°F. Generously butter and flour four 8- or 9-inch round cake pans. Combine the flour, baking powder, and salt in one medium bowl. In another, combine the raisins, pecans, cinnamon, allspice, and cloves. Use a big spoon to stir the flour mixture well, and then to mix the raisins, nuts, and spices together.

IN A LARGE BOWL, combine the butter and the sugar, and beat with a mixer at high speed to combine them well. Add the eggs one at a time, beating to make a smooth, fluffy mixture. Stir the vanilla into the milk. Add about half the flour mixture, and then half the milk, beating at low speed after each addition only to mix everything together well. Repeat with the remaining flour and milk.

DIVIDE HALF THE BATTER between 2 of the pans, and set them aside. Stir the raisins, nuts, and spices into the remaining batter. Divide this spiced batter between the 2 remaining pans, and set all 4 cake pans in the oven.

BAKE at 350°F for 20 to 25 minutes, until the layers are golden brown, pulling away from the sides of the pans, and spring back when touched lightly in the center. Cool the layers on a wire rack or a folded kitchen towel for 10 minutes, and then turn them out onto the wire racks or onto plates to cool completely, top side up.

WHILE THE CAKE IS BAKING, make the filling. In a heavy medium saucepan, bring the 1 cup of water to a boil over medium heat. Stir in the sugar, lemon juice and zest, and coconut, and bring to a boil. Adjust the heat to maintain a gentle boil, and cook for 7 minutes, stirring now and then. Mix the cornstarch into the cold water, stir well, and then add the mixture to the pan, mixing to dissolve it into the filling. Reduce the heat to a simmer and cook for 3 to 4 minutes, stirring often, until the filling is thickened and clear. Remove from the heat, transfer to a bowl, and cool to room temperature, stirring now and then.

CONTINUED

CONTINUED

Lemon-Coconut Filling

1 cup water

2 cups sugar

¼ cup lemon juice

1 tablespoon grated lemon zest

About 3½ cups freshly grated coconut (see page 57), or sweetened, shredded coconut

2 tablespoons cornstarch

½ cup cold water

TO COMPLETE THE CAKE, place a plain, unspiced layer, top side down, on a cake stand or serving plate, and poke little holes all over it so that some of the filling will penetrate the cake. Spread about one fourth of the cooled filling over the layer all the way to the edges. Place a spiced layer over the filling, poke holes all over, and spread with another quarter of the filling. Repeat with the remaining layers and filling, placing the final spiced layer top side up and pouring all the remaining filling over the layer so that a little cascades down the sides of the cake. Let stand for several hours to firm up, and cover and chill overnight. If possible, remove the cake from the refrigerator an hour or so in advance of serving time, to return to room temperature.

My mother made this simple and satisfying date-nut loaf cake each December for holiday feasting, snacking, and cookie gift plates to share with friends. She stored it wrapped in foil with thinly sliced apples inside to keep it moist. Then we had three Christmas treasures to choose from: my grandmother's coconut cake and fruitcake, which she baked for each of her daughters' families, and this fine little cake.

Mother's Date-Nut Cake

SERVES 6 TO 8

- Two 8-ounce packages (about 2 cups) whole dates
- 1¼ cups chopped pecans or walnuts
- 1 cup all-purpose flour
- 1 cup sugar
- ½ cup (1 stick) butter, melted
- 1 teaspoon vanilla extract
- 4 eggs, separated

HEAT THE OVEN to 250°F. Grease a 9-by-5-inch loaf pan generously, and line the bottom with waxed paper or kitchen parchment.

CHOP THE DATES COARSELY, and then combine them with the nuts in a large bowl. Sprinkle the flour over them and stir well, mixing the dates and nuts together and coating everything with flour. Mix in the sugar, and then add the melted butter to the bowl. Use a large spoon or a spatula to combine everything well. Add the vanilla to the egg yolks and use a fork to beat them well. Stir the egg yolks into the date mixture. The batter will be very thick and chunky.

IN A LARGE MIXING BOWL, beat the egg whites with a mixer at high speed, until they swell into a soft, puffy white cloud, shiny but not dry, 3 to 4 minutes. Add the beaten egg whites to the thick batter, and fold everything together very gently, leaving a few streaks of egg white in the batter.

SCRAPE THE BATTER into the loaf pan. Bake at 250°F for 1½ hours, until golden brown and firm, and a toothpick inserted in the center comes out clean.

COOL IN THE PAN on a wire rack or folded kitchen towel for 30 minutes. Then turn out onto a wire rack, turn top side up, and cool completely before slicing. Keep tightly wrapped in foil or in a cake tin. To season the cake, cover the top of the cake with thin slices of apple, wrap it tightly in foil, and store at room temperature for 1 week.

This luscious cake is a favorite throughout the Hispanic world and has become popular in North Carolina during the last few years. *Tres Leches* refers to the three kinds of milk that make up the sweet sauce. My friend John Whitener, an excellent cook and host, shared his version with me. John includes lime zest, which provides a bright note of citrus to temper the cake's sweetness. Tres Leches Cake is wonderful plain, and gorgeous when garnished with fresh fruit.

Johnny C's Tres Leches Cake

SERVES 8 TO 10

Cake

- 3 cups all-purpose flour
- 1 tablespoon plus 1 teaspoon baking powder
- 1 cup (2 sticks) butter, softened
- 2 cups sugar
- 4 eggs
- 1 cup milk

Three-Milk Sauce

- 1½ cups milk
- ½ cup sweetened condensed milk
- One 12-ounce can evaporated milk
- 1 tablespoon grated lime zest

Garnish

- Sweetened whipped cream for garnish (optional)
- Fresh fruit, such as kiwi fruit or berries, for garnish (optional)

TO MAKE THE CAKE, heat the oven to 350°F. Grease and flour a 13-by-9-inch pan. In a medium bowl, combine the flour and baking powder and stir with a fork to mix well.

IN A LARGE BOWL, combine the butter and sugar, and beat with a mixer at high speed to mix well. Add the eggs, one by one, beating well each time and stopping to scrape down the bowl now and then, until the mixture is light, fluffy, and smooth.

ADD ONE THIRD of the flour mixture, and then half the milk, beating at low speed each time just until the flour or milk disappears into the batter. Add another third of the flour, the remaining milk, and the remaining flour in the same way.

POUR THE BATTER into the prepared pan and bake at 350°F for 35 to 40 minutes, until the cake is golden brown, springs back when touched lightly in the center, and begins to pull away from the sides of the pan.

WHILE THE CAKE BAKES, make the sauce. Combine the milk, sweetened condensed milk, and evaporated milk in a medium saucepan. Heat gently over medium heat, stirring often, until the mixture forms a smooth, steaming hot sauce. Do not let it come to a boil.

COOL THE CAKE, in the pan, on a wire rack or folded kitchen towel for 10 minutes. Sprinkle the lime zest over the cake. Punch holes with a toothpick in the top of the cake, about 1 inch apart.

SLOWLY POUR the warm milk sauce over the warm cake in stages, stopping to let the cake absorb some of the sauce before adding more. You may not need all of the Three-Milk Sauce, and you can add more later, as the cake cools.

LET STAND for 1 hour. Cover and refrigerate, allowing the cake to come to room temperature before serving. Cut into squares and serve right from the pan. Garnish with sweetened whipped cream and fresh fruit if you like.

Christmas morning breakfast at our house always included this outstanding cake, which had enough cinnamon to perfume the kitchen and enough brown sugar and pecans to make us clamor for seconds. I love to make it throughout the year, sometimes in a tube pan but mostly in a big rectangle so that it's easy to cut into yummy, portable squares.

Mother's Cinnamon-Pecan Coffee Cake

SERVES 8 TO 10

Cinnamon-Raisin Filling

- 1½ cups light brown sugar
- 3 tablespoons all-purpose flour
- 3 tablespoons ground cinnamon
- 1½ cups raisins
- 1½ cups coarsely chopped pecans
- ¾ cup (1½ sticks) butter, melted

Coffee Cake

- 3 cups all-purpose flour
- 1 tablespoon baking powder
- 1 teaspoon salt
- 1 teaspoon vanilla extract
- 1 cup milk
- 1 cup (2 sticks) butter, softened
- 1 cup sugar
- 2 eggs

HEAT THE OVEN to 350°F, and grease and flour a 13-by-9-inch pan.

TO MAKE THE FILLING, combine the light brown sugar, flour, and cinnamon in a medium bowl, and stir with a fork to mix everything well. Combine the raisins and pecans in another bowl and toss to mix them. Place the cinnamon mixture, the nut mixture, and the melted butter by the baking pan.

TO MAKE THE COFFEE CAKE BATTER, combine the flour, baking powder, and salt in a medium bowl, and stir with a fork to mix them together well. Stir the vanilla into the milk. In a large bowl, combine the butter and the sugar, and beat with a mixer at high speed, stopping to scrape down the bowl, until pale yellow and evenly mixed, about 2 minutes. Add the eggs and beat for another 2 minutes, scraping down the bowl now and then, until the mixture is smooth and light.

USING A LARGE SPOON or a spatula, add about a third of the flour mixture to the butter mixture, and stir only until the flour disappears. Add about a third of the milk and mix it in. Repeat two more times with the remaining flour and milk, stirring just enough each time to keep the batter smooth.

SPREAD HALF THE BATTER evenly over the bottom of the prepared pan. Sprinkle half the cinnamon mixture over the batter, followed by half the melted butter. Scatter half the raisins and nuts over the batter. Spread the remaining batter carefully over the filling, using a spatula or a spoon to smooth the batter all the way to the edges of the pan. Top with the remaining cinnamon mixture, butter, and nut mixture, covering the cake evenly.

BAKE at 350°F for 45 to 50 minutes, until the cake is golden brown, fragrant, and beginning to pull away from the sides of the pan. Cool the cake in the pan for 5 to 10 minutes on wire racks or a folded kitchen towel, and then serve in squares right from the pan. The cake is delicious hot, warm, or at room temperature.

Hungry for Home: Stories of Food from Across the Carolinas is a treasure written by Amy Rogers, editor at Novello Festival Press of Charlotte, North Carolina. It is a moving and delightful collection of recipes and reminiscences gathered by Ms. Rogers from home cooks throughout the region. The book includes this lovely recipe for a holiday trifle, contributed by Marilyn Meacham Price. She cherishes a copy of this recipe handwritten by her grandmother, Alice Lenora Duke Wooten, in 1924. You will need a punch bowl, or a very large mixing bowl or salad bowl, to assemble this splendid dessert. It should be made and chilled a day in advance, and served in small bowls.

Alice Lenora Duke Wooten's Tipsey Cake

SERVES 6 TO 8

Cake

- 2½ cups all-purpose flour
- 1 teaspoon baking soda
- 1 teaspoon cream of tartar
- 3 egg whites
- 6 egg yolks
- 2 cups sugar
- 2 teaspoons vanilla extract
- 1 cup boiling water

Custard

- 8 eggs
- 2 cups sugar
- 8 cups milk

TO MAKE THE CAKE, heat the oven to 350°F. Grease and flour three 8-inch round cake pans. Combine the flour, baking soda, and cream of tartar in a medium bowl, and stir with a fork to mix them well. Beat the egg whites with a mixer at low speed until they are foamy, about 1 minute. Increase the speed to high, and beat until they billow into thick, plump clouds with soft, curling peaks. Set aside.

IN A LARGE BOWL, beat the egg yolks at medium speed just to blend them into a smooth mixture. Add the sugar and vanilla and beat until the mixture is pale, shiny, and thick, 2 to 3 minutes. Gently fold in the beaten egg whites, and then stir in the boiling water. Add the flour mixture, stir everything together well, and pour the batter into the prepared pans.

BAKE at 350°F for 20 to 25 minutes, until the cakes are golden brown and spring back when touched lightly in the center. Cool in the pans on wire racks or folded kitchen towels for 10 minutes. Then turn out onto wire racks or plates, turn right side up, and cool completely. Wrap the cooled cakes so that they are airtight until you are ready to complete the cake.

WHILE THE CAKE IS BAKING, make the custard. In a medium bowl, beat the eggs with a mixer at low speed to break them up, and then gradually beat in the sugar, scraping down the bowl occasionally. When the mixture is light colored, shiny, and thick, transfer to a large heavy saucepan. Add the milk and stir to mix everything well. Bring to a gentle boil over medium heat, stirring often, and cook for 10 to 12 minutes, until fragrant and thickened. Set aside to cool completely.

Sweetened Whipped Cream

- 1 cup heavy cream or whipping cream
- 4 cups half-and-half
- 3/4 cup sugar

To Finish the Cake

- 3 1/2 cups whole blanched almonds
- 3 cups sweet white wine, such as Riesling or sauvignon blanc
- 2 1/2 cups thinly sliced almonds

TO MAKE THE WHIPPED CREAM, beat the cream with a mixer at high speed until it swells into thick, billowy clouds and holds its shape. Combine the half-and-half and the sugar in a large bowl or pot, and stir well to dissolve the sugar. Add the whipped cream to the bowl, and stir with a whisk or a big spoon to mix everything together well.

TO FINISH THE CAKE, place one layer in the bottom of a punch bowl, or another large mixing or serving bowl. Poke about one third of the whole blanched almonds into the cake, all over the top. Drizzle about 1 cup of the wine all over the layer. Pour about one third of the custard over the cake, and sprinkle it with one third of the sliced almonds. Repeat with the second and third layers of the cake, placing each one top side up on the previous layer before adding whole almonds, wine, custard, and sliced almonds. Spread the whipped cream mixture all over the top layer, and then cover the cake and place it in the refrigerator to chill overnight. Let stand at room temperature for 1 to 2 hours before serving. Serve from the punch bowl, using a large serving spoon to cut through all the layers.

If you are fortunate enough to be invited to attend the Passover seder hosted by Ann Grundfest Gerache of Vicksburg's Congregation Anshe Chesed, be sure to save room for dessert. Her specialty is sham tart, an ethereal meringue confection covered with sweet fresh strawberries and topped off with a dollop of whipped cream. Made in muffin tins for individual portions, or in a spring-form pan for one glamorous and irresistible dessert, the dish is Mrs. Gerache's Mississippi Delta version of *schaum torte*, a classic dessert with roots in Germany and Alsace.

Maw Maw's Slip and Slide Passover Torte

SERVES 6 TO 8

As a beautiful finale made without flour, the torte is a perfect choice for the Passover feast. But the springtime temperature in Vicksburg can be mighty warm, so care must be taken that the cake stays put on its serving plate; hence the name.

- 5 egg whites
- ½ teaspoon salt
- ½ teaspoon cream of tartar
- 1½ cups sugar
- ½ teaspoon vanilla extract
- ½ teaspoon almond extract
- 2 to 3 cups fresh ripe fruit, such as strawberries, raspberries, or sliced peaches
- 2 cups sweetened whipped cream, or ice cream

HEAT THE OVEN to 450°F, and grease a 9-inch springform pan.

BEAT THE EGG WHITES with a mixer at high speed until frothy. Add the salt and cream of tartar, and then beat until the mixture blossoms into soft, shiny clouds that hold very soft peaks. Slowly add the sugar, scraping down the bowl and beating well until the mixture is stiff, but not dry, and holds a sturdy curl when the beaters are raised. Beat in the vanilla and almond extracts, and then scrape the meringue into the prepared pan.

USE A SPATULA or a large spoon to shape the torte. Build up the sides, creating a soft, thick pie shell. Bake at 450°F for 20 minutes. Then turn the oven off without opening the door, and leave the meringue shell to cool inside the oven for at least 6 hours, and as long as overnight.

TO SERVE, unmold the meringue from the springform pan, and transfer it to a cake stand or serving plate. Sweeten the fruit to your taste, and spoon it into the meringue shell. Top it off with whipped cream or softened ice cream. The finished *schaum torte* should be firm and golden on the outside, and moist on the inside.

This recipe comes from *Matzoh Ball Gumbo: Culinary Tales of the Jewish South*, by Marcie Cohen Ferris. Poignant photographs grace this extraordinary book, including a formal family portrait of Isadore and Jennie Gottlieb with their five small daughters. The couple opened Gottlieb's Bakery in Savannah in 1884, and within a decade or two, their daughter Sadie had grown up to be their master baker, renowned far and wide for her classic Southern benne cookies, praline cake, and chocolate chewie cookies, as well as her traditional pumpernickel, challah, strudel, and stollen.

Sister Sadie's Rosh Hashanah Honey Cake

SERVES 8 TO 10

Ms. Ferris kindly shared this recipe for "Sister Sadie's" honey cake, a traditional indulgence during celebrations of the Jewish New Year, when eating sweet things, especially things made with honey, sets the stage for a sweet year to come. Gottlieb's Bakery closed in 1994, but not to worry; Gottlieb's Restaurant and Dessert Bar is now open for business in Savannah, run by the new generation of Sister Sadie's family.

- 3½ cups all-purpose flour
- 2 teaspoons baking powder
- ½ teaspoon baking soda
- 1 teaspoon ground allspice
- 1 teaspoon ground cinnamon
- ½ teaspoon salt
- 2 cups honey
- 1 cup sugar
- 4 eggs
- ½ cup flat Coca-Cola or cold strong coffee
- ½ cup canola oil
- ¼ cup sliced almonds

HEAT THE OVEN to 325°F. Grease two 9-by-5-inch loaf pans. Line the pans with foil, letting the excess hang over the sides; grease the foil.

IN A LARGE BOWL, use a fork to stir together the flour, baking powder, baking soda, allspice, cinnamon, and salt.

IN A MEDIUM BOWL, beat the honey and sugar with a fork or a wooden spoon until blended. Stir in the eggs, two at a time, until well blended. Stir in the Coca-Cola or coffee and the oil, and beat to mix everything well.

POUR THE HONEY MIXTURE into the flour mixture and stir with a wooden spoon just until blended. The batter will be quite thin; a few lumps are okay. Pour the batter into the prepared pans. Sprinkle the tops with the almonds.

BAKE at 325°F until the cakes spring back when touched gently in the center and a toothpick inserted into the center comes out clean, 50 to 55 minutes. Cover lightly with foil if the almonds begin to burn. The cakes may sink slightly in the center, which is fine. Don't worry if the tops crack a bit, too. Transfer to wire racks or folded kitchen towels to cool in the pans for 30 minutes.

USING THE FOIL AS LIFTERS, remove the cakes from the pans. Carefully peel off the foil and let the cakes cool completely on the racks, almond side up. Honey cake develops flavor upon standing, and tastes better the day after baking.

LAYER CAKES, PLAIN AND FANCY

Nothing is more American than a layer cake with icing in between, and Southerners love this kind of cake more than any other. Pound cakes are elegant, cheesecakes are luscious, flourless chocolate tortes are sophisticated, and Bundt cakes are fun. But layer cakes are endearing, most especially when displayed on a pedestal cake stand in the center of a table.

This chapter gives you a repertoire of Southern specialties, from homey OATMEAL CAKE (page 95) and HUMMINGBIRD CAKE (page 106) to the ethereal CHARLESTON HUGUENOT TORTE (page 101) and a devastatingly delicious south Louisiana specialty, THIBODAUX CHOCOLATE DOBERGE CAKE (page 107). Frostings vary, from old-time chocolate and cool whipped cream to coconut-pecan, and a fabulous peanut butter icing on JAMES McNAIR'S PEANUT CAKE (page 110).

These cakes are perfect for gatherings, since each one can provide generous slices to a small crowd or decent slices for more than two dozen people, and even more if you have multiple desserts.

If you love layer cakes, invest in a set of three cake pans, either 8-inch or 9-inch, so that you can create high-rise beauties as well as the 9-inch two-layer kind we enjoyed growing up around here. If time is an issue, make the layers ahead, and wrap them well for the freezer or the refrigerator. Then you can set them out on a counter to warm up, make a wonderful frosting, and have a showstopping cake ready to share any time.

This hearty cake has been around for decades, long before any discussion of the nutritional benefits of oats. Its nubby texture is a pleasure, and since oatmeal shows up mostly at breakfast, you're allowed to take along a piece of oatmeal cake on a busy morning when you need something good to-go. The popular modern version of this classic cake is baked in a 13-by-9-inch pan and frosted with a pecan-coconut frosting, toasted in the oven to make it fragrant and crunchy-sweet. I love it as an everyday layer cake, frosted between the layers and on the top with a simple buttery white icing studded with coconut and pecans, its sides left plain to show off its handsome hue.

Oatmeal Cake

SERVES 8 TO 10

Cake

- 1 cup old-fashioned oatmeal (not quick-cooking)
- ½ cup (1 stick) butter, cut into 6 chunks
- 1½ cups boiling water
- 1½ cups all-purpose flour
- 1 teaspoon baking soda
- 1 teaspoon salt
- 1 teaspoon ground nutmeg
- 1 cup sugar
- 1 cup light brown sugar
- 2 eggs, beaten well
- 1 teaspoon vanilla extract

Coconut-Pecan Frosting

- ½ cup (1 stick) butter
- ¼ cup evaporated milk
- 1 cup sugar
- 1 teaspoon vanilla extract
- 1 cup chopped pecans
- 1 cup sweetened shredded coconut

TO MAKE THE CAKE, in a medium bowl, combine the oatmeal, butter, and boiling water, and stir to mix them together a bit. Set aside for 20 to 30 minutes.

HEAT THE OVEN to 350°F, and generously grease and flour two 9-inch round cake pans, or one 13-by-9-inch pan.

IN A MEDIUM BOWL, combine the flour, baking soda, salt, and nutmeg, and stir with a fork to mix everything well. In a large bowl, combine both kinds of sugar with the eggs and vanilla, and beat with a mixer at medium speed for about 2 minutes, stopping to scrape down the bowl, until thick and light colored.

STIR THE FLOUR MIXTURE into the egg mixture in 2 batches, beating just long enough each time to make the flour disappear. Mix in the oatmeal, stirring and folding to combine everything into a nubby but well-mixed batter.

SCRAPE INTO THE PREPARED PANS and bake at 350°F for 25 to 30 minutes, until the cakes are golden brown, spring back when touched lightly in the center, and begin pulling away from the sides of the pans. Cool in the pans on wire racks or folded kitchen towels for 10 minutes. If you have used round cake pans, carefully turn out the cakes onto wire racks, turn top side up, and finish cooling. Or cool the cake in the large rectangular pan.

TO MAKE THE FROSTING, in a medium saucepan, combine the butter, evaporated milk, and sugar, and place it over medium heat. Bring to a gentle boil, stirring now and then. Remove from the heat, and stir in the vanilla, pecans, and coconut. Beat well with a wooden spoon, a whisk, or a mixer on low speed, until you have a thickened, cooled frosting. Spread it between the two layers and then on the top of the cake, or spread it over the top of the rectangular cake, and serve it in squares, right from the pan.

Southern cooks welcome unusual ingredients in their cakes, including fruit cocktail, cola, chocolate syrup, sauerkraut, baby food, mayonnaise, zucchini, and graham cracker crumbs. Condensed tomato soup appeared on grocery shelves in 1897, and recipes for tomato soup cake were common in cookbooks by the 1930s. I love this one as a layer cake, served with a simple vanilla frosting you can make while the cake is baking; **Cream Cheese Frosting** (page 148) works, too. Southern cooks don't keep the key ingredient a mystery: we find quirkiness attractive, and tomato soup cake is pretty, easy, and simply delicious.

Tomato Soup Cake

SERVES 6 TO 8

Cake

- 2 cups all-purpose flour
- 1⅓ cups sugar
- 1 tablespoon plus 1 teaspoon baking powder
- 1½ teaspoons ground allspice
- 1 teaspoon baking soda
- 1 teaspoon ground cinnamon
- ½ teaspoon ground cloves
- One 10¾-ounce can condensed Campbell's cream of tomato soup
- ½ cup vegetable shortening or butter, softened
- 2 eggs, lightly beaten
- ¼ cup water

Vanilla Frosting

- 1 cup (2 sticks) butter
- ½ cup sugar
- ½ cup light brown sugar
- 1 cup evaporated milk
- ½ teaspoon vanilla extract
- ⅓ to ½ cup sifted confectioners' sugar

TO MAKE THE CAKE, heat the oven to 350°F, and grease and flour two 9-inch cake pans, or a 13-by-9-inch pan. In a large bowl, combine the flour, sugar, baking powder, allspice, baking soda, cinnamon, and cloves, and stir with a fork to mix everything together well. Add the tomato soup, shortening, eggs, and water to the bowl. Using a whisk or a mixer at low speed, beat all the ingredients into a smooth batter, stopping to scrape down the bowl occasionally.

SCRAPE THE BATTER into the prepared pans and bake at 350°F for about 25 minutes, until the cakes are golden brown, spring back when touched lightly in the center, and begin to pull away from the sides of the pans.

COOL IN THE PANS on wire racks or a folded kitchen towel for 10 minutes. Then, if you used round pans, turn out the cakes and place them, top side up, on the racks or on plates to cool completely. Or cool the cake in the large rectangular pan.

TO MAKE THE FROSTING, combine the butter, both kinds of sugar, and the evaporated milk in a medium saucepan, and bring to a gentle boil over medium heat. Cook for about 4 minutes, stirring often, until the sugars dissolve and the mixture thickens to a rich syrup. Remove from the heat and stir in the vanilla and confectioners' sugar. Using a large wooden spoon, whisk, or eggbeater, beat the confectioners' sugar into the frosting.

TO COMPLETE THE CAKE, place a layer, top side down, on a cake stand or serving platter, and spread frosting on the top. Place the second layer, right side up, on top. Frost the sides and then the top of the cake, or spread frosting over the rectangular top.

REFRIGERATE 30 minutes to let the frosting become firm, then serve it in squares right from the pan.

This is one simple, satisfying little cake, a standard from my mother's 1950s-era recipe box. Typed up on a big index card, the recipe has two notes I share with you: Next to the option of fresh or canned pumpkin, my mother wrote, "Fresh is best!" At the beginning of the instructions for mixing up the cake, she wrote emphatically, "Do not use mixer!" Now I find that canned pumpkin makes a beautiful cake, but I do take her advice on the issue of spoon versus mixer. It is worth the extra effort for the texture, and the recipe comes together quickly even when you're cooking unplugged. You can ice this cake while it is still warm from the oven, or wait until after it has cooled.

Pumpkin-Raisin Cake *with Lemon–Cream Cheese Frosting*

SERVES 8 TO 10

Pumpkin-Raisin Cake

- 2½ cups self-rising flour (see Note)
- 2 teaspoons ground cinnamon
- ½ teaspoon ground nutmeg
- ¾ cup raisins
- 1 cup chopped pecans or walnuts
- 1 cup plus 2 tablespoons vegetable oil
- 2 cups sugar
- 4 eggs
- 2 cups canned pumpkin or freshly cooked mashed pumpkin

Lemon–Cream Cheese Frosting

- About 3 cups confectioners' sugar
- One 8-ounce package (1 cup) cream cheese, softened
- Pinch of salt
- Juice and grated zest of 1 lemon (2 to 3 tablespoons juice and 1 tablespoon zest)
- 2 tablespoons evaporated milk, half-and-half, or milk (optional)

TO MAKE THE CAKE, heat the oven to 325°F. Grease and flour one 13-by-9-inch pan, or two 8- or 9-inch round cake pans. In a medium bowl, combine the self-rising flour with the cinnamon and nutmeg, stirring with a fork to mix everything well. In another medium bowl, combine the raisins and nuts with ¼ cup of the flour mixture and 2 tablespoons of the oils and toss to mix well.

IN A LARGE BOWL, combine the sugar and the remaining 1 cup of oil, and mix well with a wooden spoon. Add the eggs, one at a time, beating well after each addition. Add the remaining flour mixture all at once and stir just until the flour disappears into the batter. Add the pumpkin and mix thoroughly. Stir in the floured raisins and nuts, gently mix them in well, and then quickly transfer the batter to the cake pans.

BAKE at 325°F for about 25 minutes, or until the cake begins to pull away from the sides of the pan and springs back when touched lightly in the center. Cool the cake in the pan on a wire rack or folded kitchen towel for 10 minutes. Then, if you used round pans, turn the cakes out and place them, top side up, on wire racks or plates to cool completely. Or cool the cake in the large, rectangular pan.

TO MAKE THE FROSTING, combine the sugar, cream cheese, salt, and lemon juice and zest in a large bowl. Mix until creamy and smooth, and add the milk only if you need it to make the icing easy to spread.

TO COMPLETE THE CAKE, place a layer, top side down, on a cake stand or serving platter, and spread frosting on the top. Place the second layer, right side up, on top. Frost the sides and then the top of the cake, or spread frosting over the top of the rectangular cake and serve it in squares, right from the pan.

NOTE: If you don't have self-rising flour, combine 2½ teaspoons of baking powder, 1¼ teaspoon of salt, and ½ teaspoon of baking soda with 2½ cups of all-purpose flour.

This old-timey combination is simple to make and simply delicious. You may want to plan ahead so that you have ripe bananas available on your kitchen counter. You can use a mixer to cream the butter, sugar, and eggs, but be sure to stir in the flour, buttermilk, and bananas with a big spoon or a spatula—the good old-fashioned way—to keep the cake tender.

Banana Cake *with Chocolate Frosting*

SERVES 8 TO 10

Banana Cake

- 2 cups all-purpose flour
- 1 teaspoon baking soda
- 1 teaspoon baking powder
- ¼ teaspoon salt
- ¾ cup (1½ sticks) butter, softened
- 1½ cups sugar
- 3 eggs, lightly beaten
- 1 teaspoon vanilla extract
- ½ cup buttermilk (see Note)
- 1½ cups mashed ripe bananas

Chocolate Frosting

- ½ cup (1 stick) butter
- ⅓ cup cocoa
- ⅓ cup evaporated milk or half-and-half
- 4 cups sifted confectioners' sugar
- 1 teaspoon vanilla extract

TO MAKE THE CAKE, heat the oven to 350°F. Grease and flour two 9-inch round cake pans. Combine the flour, baking soda, baking powder, and salt in a medium bowl, and stir with a fork to combine well.

IN A LARGE BOWL, combine the butter and sugar, and beat well, about 2 minutes. Add the eggs, one by one, and then the vanilla. Beat well for 2 to 3 minutes more, scraping down the bowl occasionally, until you have a smooth batter.

USING A LARGE SPOON or spatula, stir in half the flour just until it disappears into the batter. Stir in the buttermilk, and then the remaining flour, the same way. Quickly and gently fold in the mashed bananas, and then divide the batter between the 2 cake pans.

BAKE at 350°F for 25 to 30 minutes, until the cakes are golden brown, spring back when touched lightly in the center, and begin to pull away from the sides of the pans.

COOL FOR 10 MINUTES in the pans on wire racks or folded kitchen towels. Then turn out onto wire racks or plates to cool completely, top side up.

TO MAKE THE FROSTING, in a medium saucepan, combine the butter, cocoa, and evaporated milk. Place over medium heat and bring to a gentle boil. Cook, stirring often, for about 5 minutes, until the cocoa dissolves into a dark, shiny essence. Remove from the heat and stir in the confectioners' sugar and vanilla. Beat with a mixer at low speed until you have a smooth, thick frosting.

TO COMPLETE THE CAKE, place one layer, top side down, on a cake plate or serving plate, and spread about 1 cup of frosting evenly over the top. Cover with the second layer, placed top side up. Spread the frosting evenly, first over the sides and then covering the top of the cake.

NOTE: If you don't have buttermilk, stir 1½ teaspoons of vinegar or lemon juice into ½ cup of milk, and let stand 10 minutes.

Carrot cake didn't come from the South, but since it got here, it has been right at home. The seventies saw carrot cakes take center stage, particularly as an alternative wedding cake. As a people who consider Jell-O to be a salad and macaroni and cheese to be a vegetable, we were quick to embrace the dubious notion that carrot cake was health food, since it had vegetables all through it and in its very name. Now we know better, but we love it still, especially with the cream cheese frosting. That counts as calcium, right?

Carrot Cake

SERVES 6 TO 8

Cake

- 2 cups all-purpose flour
- 2 teaspoons ground cinnamon
- 1½ teaspoons baking soda
- 1 teaspoon salt
- 1 cup sugar
- 1 cup light brown sugar
- 1 cup vegetable oil
- 4 eggs, lightly beaten
- 3 cups grated or finely shredded carrots (6 to 8 medium carrots)
- 1¼ cups coarsely chopped walnuts or pecans

Cream Cheese Frosting

- One 8-ounce package (1 cup) cream cheese, softened
- 3 tablespoons butter, softened
- One 1-pound box (3⅔ cups) confectioners' sugar
- 1 teaspoon vanilla extract
- 1 to 2 tablespoons milk or orange juice (optional)

TO MAKE THE CAKE, heat the oven to 350°F, and grease and flour two 9-inch round cake pans. In a medium bowl, combine the flour, cinnamon, baking soda, and salt, and stir with a fork to mix well.

IN A LARGE BOWL, combine both kinds of sugar with the oil, and stir well with a wooden spoon, or beat with a mixer at low speed, to mix them together well. Add the beaten eggs in 3 batches, mixing well after each addition. Stir in the flour in 2 batches, mixing only until the flour disappears into the batter. Fold in the carrots and the nuts, and stir gently just to combine everything.

BAKE at 350°F for 30 to 35 minutes, until the cakes are golden brown, spring back when touched lightly in the center, and begin to pull away from the sides of the pans.

COOL IN THE PANS on wire racks or on folded kitchen towels for 15 minutes, and then turn the cakes out onto cake racks or plates to cool completely.

TO MAKE THE FROSTING, combine the cream cheese and butter in a large bowl and beat well with a mixer at medium speed until soft and fluffy, 1 to 2 minutes. Add the confectioners' sugar and the vanilla, and beat to mix everything together into a smooth frosting. If it seems too stiff, beat in the milk.

TO COMPLETE THE CAKE, place a layer, top side down, on a cake stand or serving platter, and cover it with about one third of the cream cheese frosting. Place the second layer on top of the frosted layer, right side up. Frost the sides and then the top of the cake. Refrigerate the cake for 30 minutes or so to help the frosting set.

I first encountered this cake in the pages of John Martin Taylor's landmark book, *Hoppin' John's Low Country Cooking*, an essential volume for anyone hungry for deep, delicious knowledge of Southern cuisine. Based on a rustic cake known as **Ozark Pudding** (page 43), this dessert appeared in *Charleston Receipts*, the grand dame of community cookbooks, published in 1950 and still in print today. Taylor tracked down Mrs. Evelyn Florance, who developed Huguenot Torte in the 1940s for the menu of the Huguenot Tavern, then a fashionable restaurant in the center of Charleston.

Charleston Huguenot Torte

SERVES 8 TO 10

Having enjoyed a serving of **Ozark pudding** at a church supper in Galveston, Texas, during the 1930s, Mrs. Florance created her own version of this delicately delicious apple-pecan dessert. John Martin Taylor's lovely Huguenot Torte is an elegant layer cake, but you can also use a springform pan and frost the top with sweetened whipped cream. Or you can bake it in a 13-by-9-inch pan and serve it in squares with whipped cream on the side.

½ cup all-purpose flour

2¼ teaspoons baking powder

½ teaspoon salt

3 eggs

1 teaspoon vanilla extract

1½ cups sugar

1¾ cups finely chopped pecans

1½ cups finely chopped apples

About 3 cups sweetened whipped cream

Pecan halves for garnish

HEAT THE OVEN to 325°F. Grease two 9-inch round cake pans generously and line them with circles of waxed paper or kitchen parchment. Grease the paper and then dust the pans with flour.

COMBINE the flour, baking powder, and salt in a small bowl and mix well with a fork. In a medium bowl, beat the eggs with a mixer at high speed for 5 to 7 minutes, until they blossom into a thick, bright yellow mixture. Add the vanilla, and then continue beating while you slowly pour in the sugar, scraping down the bowl often. Beat well until the mixture is very thick, shiny, and almost tripled in volume, 3 to 5 minutes more.

FINISH MIXING THE CAKE with a wooden spoon or spatula instead of a mixer. Sprinkle the flour mixture over the egg mixture, followed by the ground nuts and the chopped apples. Gently fold these ingredients into the egg mixture to make a nubby and delicate, but well mixed batter.

DIVIDE THE BATTER between the 2 prepared pans, and bake at 325°F for 30 to 35 minutes, until the cakes are golden brown and begin to pull away from the sides of the pans. Don't touch the center of the cakes as they will be quite fragile. Transfer the cakes to wire racks or folded kitchen towels to cool completely in the pans.

CONTINUED

CONTINUED

TO COMPLETE THE CAKE, very carefully invert each cooled cake layer onto a wire rack or a plate, remove the waxed paper, and turn right side up. Place one layer on a cake stand or serving plate, top side down, and frost it generously with half the sweetened whipped cream. Cover with the second layer, top side up, spread the remaining whipped cream over the top, and place the pecan halves on the whipped cream. Chill for at least 30 minutes and serve.

Nobody knows for sure where this cake comes from, but lots of people agree with me that it is one magnificent cake. Its signature carmine coloration is dazzling, and I adore its tangy little grace note of flavor, created by the unusual combination of vinegar, buttermilk, and cocoa in the batter. Red food coloring is the not-so-secret ingredient responsible for its sassy color. Try gel paste food coloring (see Sur La Table or Sweet Celebrations, page 162) if you'd like to experiment with another route to red.

Red Velvet Cake

SERVES 8 TO 10

Cake

- 2½ cups all-purpose flour
- ½ teaspoon salt
- 1 teaspoon vanilla extract
- 1 cup buttermilk (see Note)
- 2 tablespoons cocoa
- One 1-ounce bottle (2 tablespoons) red food coloring
- 1 cup (2 sticks) butter, softened
- 2 cups sugar
- 2 eggs
- 1½ teaspoons baking soda
- 1 tablespoon cider vinegar or white vinegar

TO MAKE THE CAKE, heat the oven to 350°F. Grease two 9-inch round cake pans generously, and line them with waxed paper or kitchen parchment. Grease the paper and flour the pans.

PREPARE THREE SEPARATE MIXTURES for the batter: Combine the flour and salt in a medium bowl and use a fork to mix them together well. Stir the vanilla into the buttermilk. Combine the cocoa and the red food coloring in a small bowl, mashing and stirring them together to make a thick, smooth paste.

IN A LARGE BOWL, beat the butter with a mixer at low speed for 1 minute, until creamy and soft. Add the sugar, and then beat well for 3 to 4 minutes, stopping to scrape down the bowl now and then. Add the eggs, one at a time, beating after each one, until the mixture is creamy, fluffy, and smooth. Scrape the cocoa–food coloring paste into the batter and beat to mix it in evenly.

ADD ABOUT A THIRD of the flour mixture, and then about half the milk, beating the batter with a mixer at low speed, and mixing only enough to make the flour or liquid disappear into the batter. Mix in another third of the flour, the rest of the milk, and then the last of the flour in the same way.

IN A SMALL BOWL, combine the baking soda and vinegar and stir well. Use a wooden spoon or spatula to quickly mix this last mixture into the red batter, folding it in gently by hand. Scrape the batter into the prepared pans.

BAKE at 350°F for 20 to 25 minutes, until the layers spring back when touched lightly in the center and are just beginning to pull away from the sides of the pans.

COOL THE CAKES in the pans on wire racks or folded kitchen towels for 15 minutes. Then turn them out on the racks or on plates, remove the paper, and turn top side up to cool completely.

CONTINUED

CONTINUED

Coconut-Pecan Icing

- 1 cup milk
- 2 tablespoons all-purpose flour
- 1 cup (2 sticks) butter, softened
- 1 cup sugar
- 1 teaspoon vanilla extract
- 1 cup sweetened shredded coconut
- 1 cup finely chopped pecans or walnuts

TO MAKE THE ICING, combine the milk and flour in a small or medium saucepan. Cook over medium heat, whisking or stirring often, until the mixture thickens almost to a paste, 2 to 4 minutes. Remove from the heat and scrape it into a small bowl to cool completely.

MEANWHILE, beat the butter with a mixer at high speed until light and fluffy. Add the sugar in thirds, beating well each time, until the mixture is creamy and fairly smooth. Add the cooled milk-and-flour mixture and beat for 1 to 2 minutes, scraping down the sides now and then, to combine everything well. Using a large spoon or your spatula, stir in the vanilla, coconut, and pecans, mixing to combine everything well into a thick, fluffy, nubby icing.

TO COMPLETE THE CAKE, place one layer, top side down, on a cake stand or a serving plate, and spread icing on the top. Place the second layer, right side up, on top. Frost the sides and then the top of the cake. Refrigerate for 30 minutes or more to help the icing set.

NOTE: If you don't have buttermilk, stir 1 tablespoon of vinegar or lemon juice into 1 cup of milk and let stand for 10 minutes.

Hummingbird cake is a modern classic that showed up in community cookbooks in North Carolina in the early '70s, and achieved stardom after it was featured as a reader's recipe in *Southern Living* magazine in 1978. It has been captivating people around the country ever since. Wonderfully rich and pretty in an understated way, it features delicious layers moistened by pineapple and bananas, and a yummy cream cheese frosting studded with pecans. It's all the more impressive for the fact that it is quite simple to make. Stir together the ingredients with a wooden spoon, and you'll have the cake in the oven in a few minutes' time. If you want to skip the frosting, you can spread the layers with sweetened whipped cream.

Hummingbird Cake

SERVES 6 TO 8

Cake

- 3 cups all-purpose flour
- 2 cups sugar
- 1 teaspoon ground cinnamon
- 1 teaspoon baking soda
- ½ teaspoon salt
- 3 eggs, slightly beaten
- ¾ cup vegetable oil
- 1½ teaspoons vanilla extract
- One 8-ounce can crushed pineapple (do not drain)
- 2 cups mashed ripe bananas
- 1 cup finely chopped pecans

Pecan–Cream Cheese Frosting

- One 8-ounce package (1 cup) cream cheese, softened
- ¼ cup (½ stick) butter, softened
- One 16-ounce box (about 3⅔ cups) confectioners' sugar
- 1 teaspoon vanilla extract
- ½ cup finely chopped pecans

TO MAKE THE CAKE, heat the oven to 350°F. Grease and flour three 8-inch or two 9-inch round cake pans and set aside. Combine the flour, sugar, cinnamon, baking soda, and salt in a large bowl, and use a fork to mix well.

WITH A LARGE WOODEN SPOON, mix in the beaten eggs, oil, vanilla, pineapple, bananas, and pecans. Mix well, stirring gently just enough to blend everything into a good, thick, nubby batter.

DIVIDE THE BATTER evenly among the cake pans and bake at 350°F for 20 to 25 minutes, until the cakes are nicely browned and pulling away from the sides of the pans.

COOL THE CAKES in the pans on wire racks or folded kitchen towels for about 15 minutes. Then gently turn out the cakes onto wire racks or plates. Turn the layers top side up, and let them cool completely.

TO MAKE THE FROSTING, in a medium bowl, combine the cream cheese and butter and beat with a mixer at low speed to mix well. Add the confectioners' sugar and vanilla and beat until the frosting is fluffy and smooth, stopping once or twice to scrape down the bowl and blend everything thoroughly. Add the pecans, and stir well.

TO COMPLETE THE CAKE, place one layer, top side down, on a cake stand or a serving plate, and spread frosting on the top. Place the second layer, top side up, on the first. Frost the sides and then the top. Refrigerate the cake for 30 minutes or so, to help the icing set.

This magnificent cake is a signature confection of the sweet and precious city of New Orleans. Known as Doberge cake (say "do-bosh"), its inspiration is the Hungarian classic Dobos torte, seven thin layers of yellow cake sandwiched together with a chocolate custard filling and finished with a chocolate frosting. In this version, from *Louisiana Legacy*, an outstanding community cookbook published in 1982 by the Service League of Thibodaux, Louisiana, the cake layers are chocolate as well. Start the cake a day before serving so it has time to firm up. For a quicker frosting, use **Blanche's Never-Fail Chocolate Icing** (page 154).

Thibodaux Chocolate Doberge Cake

SERVES 8 TO 10

Chocolate Doberge Cake

- 2 cups sifted all-purpose flour
- 1 teaspoon baking soda
- 1 teaspoon salt
- Three 1-ounce squares unsweetened chocolate
- 10 tablespoons (1¼ sticks) butter, softened
- 1½ cups sugar
- 3 eggs, separated
- 1 cup buttermilk (see Note)
- 1¼ teaspoons vanilla extract
- 1 teaspoon almond extract

TO MAKE THE CAKE, heat the oven to 300°F. Grease two 9-inch round cake pans generously and flour them. Into a medium bowl, sift together the flour, baking soda, and salt 3 times.

BRING ABOUT 3 INCHES OF WATER to a simmer in the bottom of a double boiler or a saucepan that will accommodate a medium heat-proof bowl so that it sits snugly above the water. Melt the chocolate in the top of the double boiler or in the bowl over the simmering water.

IN A LARGE BOWL, combine the butter and the sugar, and beat with a mixer at high speed to combine them well. Add the egg yolks and continue beating, stopping to scrape down the bowl, until light, smooth, and fluffy, 2 to 3 minutes. Add about one third of the flour mixture, and then one third of the buttermilk, mixing after each addition only enough to make the flour or liquid disappear into the batter. Repeat 2 more times with the remaining flour and buttermilk. Add the melted chocolate and beat at low speed to combine everything well.

IN A MEDIUM BOWL, beat the egg whites at high speed until they are stiff but not dry, and hold a sturdy curl when the beaters are lifted. Use a large spoon or a spatula to fold them gently into the batter, along with the vanilla and almond extracts.

DIVIDE THE BATTER between the prepared pans, and bake at 300°F for 35 to 40 minutes, or until each cake springs back when touched lightly in the center and begins to pull away from the sides of the pan. Cool for 10 minutes in the pans on wire racks or folded kitchen towels. Then turn out the cakes onto wire racks or plates to cool completely, top side up. After the cakes cool, carefully slice each one in half horizontally. Place one hand on top of a cake to steady it, and using a gentle sawing motion, cut it crosswise into 2 thin layers with a long, serrated knife. Repeat with the second cake.

CONTINUED

CONTINUED

Don't separate the layers until you are ready to fill and frost them.

TO MAKE THE FILLING, combine the evaporated milk and chocolate in a medium saucepan and cook over medium heat until the chocolate melts. In a medium bowl, combine the sugar and flour, stirring with a fork to mix well. Gradually add about 1 cup of the chocolate mixture to the sugar-and-flour mixture, stirring to make a smooth paste. Scrape the chocolate-and-sugar mixture into the saucepan, and cook over medium heat until it thickens, 2 to 3 minutes. Carefully and quickly stir about ⅓ cup of the chocolate mixture into the egg yolks to warm them. Then add the warmed egg yolks to the saucepan and stir well to mix them into the filling quickly. Cook for 2 to 3 minutes more, until the filling is thick, shiny, and smooth. Remove from the heat, add the butter and the vanilla and almond extracts, and stir to mix everything well. Cool to room temperature.

TO MAKE THE FROSTING, combine the sugar, evaporated milk, and chocolate in a heavy saucepan. Stir to mix them together, and then bring to a gentle boil over medium heat, stirring almost constantly. Reduce the heat to maintain a gentle but lively simmer, and cook the shiny, bubbling mixture without stirring for 6 minutes. Add the butter and vanilla, and cook on medium heat for 1 to 2 minutes more, stirring often, until the mixture is thick and smooth. Set aside to cool for 20 to 30 minutes, until the mixture is lukewarm. (Transfer to a bowl and place in the refrigerator if you need to speed things up.)

TO FILL THE CAKE, place one thin layer, top side down, on a cake stand or serving plate, and spread about 1 cup of the chocolate filling evenly over the surface. Cover with the other half of the same cake, bottom side up, and spread it with another cup of the filling. Continue with the third thin layer, placing it bottom side down and covering it with the remaining filling. Place the fourth thin layer on the filled cake, top side up, leaving it plain. Set aside for at least 30 minutes to firm up; or cover and refrigerate for several hours.

TO COMPLETE THE CAKE, beat the cooled frosting well, and spread it over the top and sides of the cake. It will be soft and creamy. Let the cake stand for several hours, or refrigerate overnight. If refrigerated, set the cake out about 2 hours before serving to allow it to come to room temperature.

NOTE: If you don't have buttermilk, stir 1 tablespoon of vinegar or lemon juice into 1 cup of milk and let stand for 10 minutes.

Chocolate Filling

2½ cups evaporated milk

Two 1-ounce squares semisweet chocolate

1¼ cups sugar

5 tablespoons all-purpose flour

4 egg yolks, lightly beaten

2 tablespoons butter

1¼ teaspoons vanilla extract

¼ teaspoon almond extract

Chocolate Frosting

1¼ cups sugar

1 cup evaporated milk or half-and-half

1½ squares unsweetened chocolate (1-ounce squares), chopped

¼ cup (½ stick) butter

1 teaspoon vanilla extract

My good friend James McNair, prolific and brilliant cookbook author, grew up in Louisiana and is the author of *James McNair's Cakes*. Ever generous, he shared this fabulous creation with me, as well as the story behind it:

"Many miles and years away from our Louisiana hometown, my sister's enormous blue eyes still sparkle when she recalls the peanut cake that we made as an after-school treat in the 1950s. I added peanut butter to a batter made from a yellow cake mix.

James McNair's Peanut Cake

SERVES 10 TO 12

While it baked, Martha and I went to Mr. Burk's service station on the corner across from the church and bought several little bags of salted peanuts, the kind you sometimes poured into bottles of 'Co-Cola' in those days. I substituted peanut butter for the butter in a cream cheese frosting recipe, and we chopped those salty nuts and pressed them all over the cake. Here's the big, moist version of that youthful memory that I made recently for Martha's birthday. Be certain to use a creamy homogenized peanut butter, not a 'natural' version."

Peanut Cake

- 4 eggs
- 1 cup whole milk
- ¼ cup peanut oil or vegetable oil
- 2 teaspoons vanilla extract
- 3 cups all-purpose flour
- 1 tablespoon baking powder
- ½ teaspoon salt
- 2 cups sugar
- ½ cup (1 stick) butter, softened
- ½ cup creamy peanut butter

TO MAKE THE CAKE, heat the oven to 350°F. Grease two 9-inch round cake pans and line the bottoms with rounds of kitchen parchment. Set aside. In a medium bowl, combine the eggs, milk, oil, and vanilla and whisk to blend well. Set aside.

COMBINE the flour, baking powder, and salt in a large bowl, and stir with a fork to mix well. Add the sugar and use a mixer at low speed or a fork to mix these dry ingredients together well, about 30 seconds. Add the butter and peanut butter and beat at medium speed until the mixture resembles coarse bread crumbs, about 45 seconds. Add about 1¼ cups of the milk mixture and beat at medium speed for 1½ minutes, and then stop and scrape down the sides of the bowl. Add the remaining milk mixture, beat for 30 seconds, stop and scrape down the sides of the bowl, and beat again until creamy smooth, about 30 seconds more.

DIVIDE THE BATTER evenly between the prepared pans and smooth the surfaces with a rubber spatula. Bake at 350°F for 25 to 30 minutes, until the cakes spring back when touched gently in the center and a wooden skewer inserted in the center comes out clean.

COOL THE CAKES in the pans on wire racks or folded kitchen towels for 5 to 10 minutes. Then turn out the cakes onto the racks to cool completely, top side up.

Peanutty Frosting

- 3/4 cup creamy peanut butter
- Two 8-ounce packages (2 cups) cream cheese
- 2 teaspoons vanilla extract
- 1/8 teaspoon salt
- One 1-pound box (about 3 2/3 cups) confectioners' sugar, sifted
- 2 to 3 tablespoons milk
- 1 1/2 cups chopped lightly salted roasted peanuts

TO MAKE THE FROSTING, put the peanut butter in a large bowl and beat with a mixer at medium speed until soft and fluffy. Add the cream cheese, vanilla, and salt and beat at low speed just until the mixture is smooth and creamy, about 1 minute; avoid overbeating, which makes the cream cheese too thin and runny. Add about half the confectioners' sugar, and beat at low speed just until it disappears into the mixture. Add the remaining confectioners' sugar and the 2 tablespoons of milk and beat just until smooth and spreadable; add a little more milk if the mixture is too thick.

TO COMPLETE THE CAKE, slice each layer horizontally in half with a long serrated knife to create a total of 4 thin layers. Place one layer, top side down, in the center of a cake stand or serving plate. Spoon about 3/4 cup of the frosting onto the cake layer and spread evenly to cover it. Place a second layer, bottom side down, on top of the frosted one and spread with another 3/4 cup of the frosting. Repeat with a third layer, bottom side down, and place the fourth layer over it, top side up. Frost the sides, and then the top of the cake, spreading the frosting evenly all over. Cover the sides of the cake with the chopped peanuts, pressing lightly to help them adhere to the frosting.

EVERYDAY CAKES FROM THE SEA ISLANDS TO THE SMOKIES

This chapter is your cook's tour of home-style baking in the nooks and crannies of the South. From the warm Atlantic coastal waters to the chilly mountain streams of the Blue Ridge, people have been baking cakes for centuries—cakes that evoke the particular places and ways of life in each distinct region.

Start with the Sea Islands off the coasts of South Carolina and Georgia. Indulge in a tender slice of fresh PEAR BREAD (page 114) from Mrs. Cornelia Walker Bailey of Sapelo Island, Georgia. Mrs. Bailey traces her family's life on Sapelo Island back to the early 1800s, and keeps the ancestors and the Geechee traditions vivid through her writing, cooking, and storytelling. Travel on up to South Carolina's Daufuskie Island, where Sallie Anne Robinson shares her comforting CARROT CAKE (page 118), along with delicious stories of Gullah traditions. Then head up to Ocracoke Island, on the Outer Banks of North Carolina, for a thick slice of FIG CAKE WITH BUTTERMILK GLAZE (page 117).

Take in a breath of Blue Ridge mountain air with a big hunk of BLACKBERRY JAM CAKE WITH CARAMEL GLAZE (page 122), or a very tall, spice-filled aromatic slice of ALLEGHANY COUNTY MOLASSES STACK CAKE (page 128), made with apples and lots of spice. You may have a hankering for a little slice of LOUISIANA SYRUP CAKE (page 120), a homey Cajun treat made with pure cane syrup, or a satisfying little square of PERSIMMON PUDDING (page 121) from the North Carolina woods. Savor it on a cool fall day, when the wild persimmons have ripened, with a dollop of sweet cream and a glass of cider.

Go see the places these cakes come from if you can. But if you can't make it out of town today or tomorrow, maybe you can sneak in a little cook's tour by baking up one or two of these cakes.

This spice-infused tea bread comes from the kitchen of Mrs. Cornelia Walker Bailey, historian, muse, and guardian angel of Sapelo Island, off the Georgia coast. Mrs. Bailey's family has lived on Sapelo Island since the year 1806, and her life's work is keeping their stories and wisdom alive and well. She works through words, telling stories, writing books, and sharing recipes for the food that has fed her ancestors for more than two hundred years.

Cornelia Walker Bailey's Pear Bread

SERVES 6 TO 8

This one comes from a book she wrote with Yvonne J. Grovner and William "Doc Bill" Thomas: *The Foods of Georgia's Barrier Islands: A Gourmet Food Guide to Native American, Geechee and European Influences on the Golden Isles*. You can make this in a tube pan as a spice cake, or in two loaf pans as a tea bread.

- 3 cups all-purpose flour
- 1 teaspoon baking soda
- ¼ teaspoon baking powder
- 1 teaspoon salt
- 1 tablespoon ground cinnamon
- 1 cup chopped walnuts
- ¾ cup (1½ sticks) butter, softened, or ¾ cup vegetable oil
- 3 eggs, lightly beaten
- 2 cups sugar
- 2 cups peeled and finely grated ripe but firm pears
- 2 teaspoons vanilla extract

HEAT THE OVEN to 350°F, and lightly grease and flour a 10-inch tube pan or two 9-by-5-inch loaf pans.

COMBINE the flour, baking soda, baking powder, salt, and cinnamon in a large mixing bowl, and stir with a fork to mix everything well. Scoop out about ¼ cup of the flour mixture and combine it in a small bowl with the chopped walnuts, stirring and tossing to coat the nuts with the flour.

IN A MEDIUM BOWL, combine the butter or oil, eggs, sugar, chopped pears, and vanilla, and stir to mix everything well. Scrape the pear mixture into the flour mixture, and stir just until the flour disappears and the batter is evenly moistened.

QUICKLY SCRAPE THE BATTER into the prepared pans, and bake at 350°F for 60 to 70 minutes, or until the bread is handsomely browned and firm on top, and a wooden skewer inserted in the center comes out clean.

COOL THE BREAD in the pan on a wire rack or folded kitchen towel for about 10 minutes. Then turn it out onto a plate or a wire rack to cool completely, top side up. Serve as is, sprinkle with confectioners' sugar, or ice with a simple frosting, such as **Buttermilk Glaze** (see page 117).

This signature cake makes use of the luscious figs that ripen in midsummer on this barrier island in North Carolina's Outer Banks. Most local residents have a backyard tree or two, and many are dedicated to eating what they can through the season, while putting an abundant portion of the crop into jars of jam and preserves.

This cake is also popular as a layer cake, filled and topped with **Cream Cheese Frosting** (page 148). For the figs, the best choice is whole preserved ones, which you drain, stem, and chop into small but signifcant chunks. Another option is dried figs, which you can stem, halve lengthwise, and simmer for 30 minutes in 1 cup of water mixed with 1 cup of sugar, and then cool and chop.

Ocracoke Island Fig Cake *with Buttermilk Glaze*

SERVES 8 TO 10

Fig Cake

- 3 eggs
- 1½ cups sugar
- 1 cup oil
- 2 cups all-purpose flour
- 1 teaspoon ground nutmeg
- 1 teaspoon ground allspice
- 1 teaspoon ground cinnamon
- 1 teaspoon salt
- 1 teaspoon baking soda dissolved in a little hot water
- ½ cup buttermilk (see Note)
- 1 teaspoon vanilla extract
- 1 cup coarsely chopped preserved figs, or fig jam
- 1 cup coarsely chopped pecans or walnuts

Buttermilk Glaze

- ½ cup buttermilk (see Note)
- ½ cup sugar
- ¼ cup (½ stick) butter
- 1½ teaspoons cornstarch or flour
- ¼ teaspoon baking soda
- 1 teaspoon vanilla extract

TO MAKE THE CAKE, heat the oven to 350°F. Grease and flour a 10-inch tube pan and set aside. Beat the eggs well until light yellow and smooth. Add the sugar and oil and continue beating well to make a thick, smooth batter.

COMBINE the flour with the nutmeg, allspice, cinnamon, and salt in a small bowl, and stir with a fork to mix well. Add half the flour mixture to the egg-and-sugar mixture and stir with a wooden spoon to blend well. Add the buttermilk and mix well. Add the remaining flour along with the baking soda dissolved in water and the vanilla, and stir to mix everything into a fairly smooth batter. Gently stir in the figs and the nuts, mixing just until they are evenly distributed throughout the batter.

QUICKLY SCRAPE THE BATTER into the prepared pan, and bake at 350°F for 40 to 50 minutes until the cake is handsomely brown and firm on top, and until a wooden skewer inserted in the center comes out clean. While the cake bakes, prepare the buttermilk glaze and set aside until the cake is done.

COOL THE CAKE in the pan on a wire rack or folded kitchen towel for about 15 minutes. Loosen the cake from the pan gently, running a table knife around the sides of the pan, and then gently turn it out onto the wire rack. Turn the cake top side up, and carefully place it on a serving plate or cake stand.

WHILE THE CAKE IS BAKING, make the glaze in a medium saucepan, combining the buttermilk, sugar, butter, cornstarch, and baking soda, and bringing to a gentle boil. Remove at once, stir well, and cool to room temperature. Add the vanilla, and set aside until the cake is done. Spoon the buttermilk glaze over the warm cake, and cool completely.

NOTE: If you don't have buttermilk, stir 1 tablespoon of vinegar or lemon juice into 1 cup of milk, and let stand for 10 minutes.

This moist cake is a celebration of fruits and vegetables, and sugar and spice. The pineapple and raisins, shredded carrots, nuts, and a small shower of spices give it flavor galore, just the way Sallie Anne Robinson likes it. Born and raised on Daufuskie Island, off the South Carolina coast, Ms. Robinson is the author of *Gullah Home Cooking the Daufuskie Way: Smokin' Joe Butter Beans, Ol' 'Fuskie Fried Crab Rice, Sticky Bush Blackberry Dumpling, and Other Sea Island Favorites*. A memoir as well as a treasury of traditional recipes, her book opens a window on Daufuskie Island life, with poignant photographs to season the stories.

Sallie Ann Robinson's Daufuskie Island Carrot Cake

SERVES 6 TO 8

1½ cups grated carrots (3 or 4 medium carrots)
1 cup golden raisins
1 cup chopped walnuts
Two 8-ounce cans (2 cups) crushed pineapple (do not drain)
1¾ cups all-purpose flour
1½ cups sugar
1 teaspoon baking soda
1 teaspoon baking powder
1 teaspoon salt
1 teaspoon ground cinnamon
¾ teaspoon ground cloves
¾ teaspoon freshly grated nutmeg
¾ teaspoon ground allspice
3 eggs, beaten
½ cup vegetable oil
⅓ cup honey
¼ cup (½ stick) butter, softened
1½ tablespoons lemon juice or orange juice

HEAT THE OVEN to 350°F, and generously grease and flour a 13-by-9-inch pan.

IN A MEDIUM BOWL, combine the carrots, raisins, walnuts, and pineapple, and stir to mix everything well. In another medium bowl, combine the flour, sugar, baking soda, baking powder, salt, cinnamon, cloves, nutmeg, and allspice, and stir with a fork to mix them well.

BREAK THE EGGS into a large bowl and stir with a fork or a whisk until they are foamy. Stir in the oil, honey, butter, and lemon juice, and mix to combine everything well. Add the flour mixture and then the carrot mixture, stirring gently with a large spoon or a spatula just until the flour disappears and the carrot mixture is fairly well incorporated into the batter.

SCRAPE THE BATTER into the pan. Bake at 350°F for 35 to 45 minutes, until the cake is golden brown and beginning to pull away from the sides of the pan, and a toothpick or a wooden skewer inserted in the center comes out clean. Cool to room temperature in the pan on a wire rack or folded kitchen towel. Cut in squares and serve right from the pan.

This recipe makes a lot from a little and yields a batch of moist, fragrant cake perfect for a snack while reading by the fireplace, hiking through the woods, or picnicking at a rest stop along the interstate during a long road trip. Cornelia Walker Bailey, author of *God, Dr. Buzzard, and the Bolito Man*, remembers her mother stirring up a pan of hard time cake, creating a delicious and nourishing treat for her family out of what she had handy: molasses, flour, spices, a dab of butter, and an abundance of love.

Sapelo Island Hard Time Cake

SERVES 8 TO 10

- 1½ cups self-rising flour (see Note)
- ¼ teaspoon ground cinnamon
- ¼ teaspoon ground cloves
- 1 cup molasses
- 1 tablespoon butter, melted
- 1 teaspoon baking soda
- ⅔ cup warm water

HEAT THE OVEN to 350°F. Lightly grease a 9-inch square or round pan.

IN A MEDIUM BOWL, combine the flour, cinnamon, and cloves and stir with a fork to mix well. Add the molasses and melted butter and use a large wooden spoon to mix everything into a thick, smooth batter. Stir the baking soda into the warm water, and then add it to the bowl, stirring until the batter is smooth and thin. Quickly pour it into the prepared pan.

BAKE at 350°F for 25 to 30 minutes, until the cake is a deep, handsome, shiny brown, springs back when touched lightly in the middle, and a toothpick inserted in the center comes out clean.

COOL IN THE PAN to room temperature on a wire rack or folded kitchen towel. Cut the cake and serve right from the pan.

NOTE: If you don't have self-rising flour, combine 1½ cups of all-purpose flour with 1½ teaspoons of baking powder, ⅝ teaspoon of baking soda, and ¾ teaspoon of salt.

This Creole confection, known also as *gâteau au sirop*, calls for pure cane syrup, a milder, more delicate cousin of molasses. Steen's pure cane syrup, still made the traditional way in Abbeville, Louisiana, is the classic choice, but you could also use maple syrup, sorghum, or a combination of any two of these sweet essences. Cane syrup provides this single cake layer with a gorgeously deep, golden hue. You could crown it with a generous dusting of confectioners' sugar, or finish it with this syrup-kissed frosting. Steen's is the real deal, proudly serving south Louisiana and the world from their syrup mill in Vermilion Parish, Louisiana, since 1911.

Louisiana Syrup Cake

SERVES 6 TO 8

TO MAKE THE CAKE, heat the oven to 350°F. Grease and flour a 9-inch square or round pan. In a medium bowl, combine the flour, cinnamon, ginger, cloves, and salt, and stir with a fork to mix everything well.

IN A LARGE BOWL, combine the vegetable oil, cane syrup, and egg, and stir with a fork or a whisk to combine everything well. Add about one third of the flour mixture to the syrup mixture, and then stir gently, just until the flour disappears. Add the baking soda to the hot water, and then stir about half the water into the batter. Stir in another third of the flour mixture, then the remaining water, and finally the remaining flour, stirring gently each time just to mix everything well.

QUICKLY POUR THE BATTER into the prepared pan, and bake at 350°F for 30 to 35 minutes, until the cake springs back when touched gently in the center, and is beginning to pull away from the sides of the pan.

SERVE WARM, right from the pan. If you've used a round pan, cool the cake in the pan on a rack or a folded kitchen towel for 10 minutes, turn it out of the pan, and place it, top side up, on a wire rack to cool completely.

TO MAKE THE FROSTING, in a medium bowl, beat the butter until light and fluffy. Add half the confectioners' sugar, the vanilla, and the salt, and beat with a mixer at medium speed until smooth. Add the remaining confectioners' sugar and the cane syrup, and beat until smooth and creamy, stopping to scrape down the bowl and mix well.

TO COMPLETE THE CAKE, if it's round, place the cooled cake on a serving plate or cake stand, top side up, and spread the frosting over it generously, covering the top and sides. If it's square, spread the icing over the cooled cake right in the pan, and cut into squares to serve.

Cake

- 2½ cups all-purpose flour
- 1 teaspoon ground cinnamon
- 1 teaspoon ground ginger
- ½ teaspoon ground cloves
- ½ teaspoon salt
- ½ cup vegetable oil
- 1½ cups Steen's pure cane syrup (see page 162)
- 1 egg
- 1½ teaspoons baking soda
- ¾ cup hot water

Cane Syrup Frosting

- ¼ cup (½ stick) butter, softened
- 2 cups sifted confectioners' sugar
- 1 teaspoon vanilla extract
- ¼ teaspoon salt
- 2 tablespoons Steen's pure cane syrup or maple syrup

North Carolina is a good place to find a wild persimmon tree, but then so are most of its neighboring states with a foothold in the Blue Ridge and Great Smoky Mountains. The trees greet winter bursting with short, round, and plump little fruits not much bigger than an oversize cherry and a fine golden-orange color when ripe and ready for picking. The fruit aren't harvested or prepared easily, being wild, popular with birds, and half-full of seeds. They seem to move from underripe to squishy in a matter of minutes.

Persimmon Pudding

SERVES 8 TO 10

Did I mention that they remain too astringent to eat without cooking? Why bother, one might ask, if one had never had old-time persimmon pudding, or not loved it as I do. It's a very moist, dense cake, somewhere between fudge and cake in texture and with a taste exactly like the colors of fall.

Pass ripe persimmons, wild or cultivated, through a colander or a food mill to get rid of their seeds and skin. Cultivated persimmons yield a lovely, milder version of this homespun classic dish, and a puree of sweet potatoes or pumpkin works nicely, too.

2 cups all-purpose flour

1½ cups sugar

1 teaspoon ground cinnamon

1 teaspoon baking soda

¼ teaspoon salt

2 cups persimmon pulp
(about 2 pounds ripe persimmons)

1¾ cups milk

2 eggs

¼ cup (½ stick) butter, melted

HEAT THE OVEN to 350°F. Generously grease a 13-by-9-inch pan. Combine the flour, sugar, cinnamon, baking soda, and salt in a medium bowl and use a fork to mix them together very well.

IN A LARGE BOWL, combine the persimmon pulp, milk, eggs, and melted butter, and stir with a whisk or fork to mix them together well. Add the flour to the persimmon mixture and stir with a whisk or wooden spoon, or fold with a spatula to mix everything into a smooth batter.

POUR THE BATTER into the prepared pan, and bake at 350°F for 40 to 50 minutes, until the cake springs back when touched gently in the center and is beginning to pull away from the sides of the pan.

PLACE THE PAN on a wire rack or a folded kitchen towel, and cool the cake completely. Cut into squares, and serve plain or with sweetened whipped cream.

With its foundation of blackberry jam, this homey spice cake delivers a postcard from last summer's berry patch. Jam cakes are traditional throughout the South, particularly in the Appalachian mountain regions of Kentucky and Tennessee. Jewel-like jars of homemade blackberry jam and strawberry preserves still provide some families with sustenance and the makings of a celebration all winter long.

Blackberry Jam Cake *with Caramel Glaze*

SERVES 6 TO 8

Caramel icing is the classic jam cake finish, but consider making this a jelly cake instead. A jelly cake is any kind of layer cake that is iced with jelly or jam; the sides are usually left plain. To finish this cake with jam or jelly, simply spread about ¾ cup of softened blackberry jam, pear preserves, or grape jelly over each layer of the cake and stack the layers, spreading a little extra jam on the top layer for a beautiful finish.

Jam Cake

- 3 cups all-purpose flour
- 2 teaspoons baking soda
- 1 teaspoon ground cinnamon
- ½ teaspoon ground allspice
- ¼ teaspoon ground cloves
- 1 cup (2 sticks) butter, softened
- 2 cups sugar
- 3 eggs
- 1½ cups blackberry, raspberry, strawberry, or pear jam at room temperature
- ¼ cup milk

TO MAKE THE CAKE, heat the oven to 350°F. Grease and flour three 8-inch or two 9-inch round cake pans. In a medium bowl, combine the flour, baking soda, cinnamon, allspice, and cloves, and stir with a fork to mix everything well.

IN A LARGE BOWL, combine the butter and sugar and beat with a mixer at high speed until very well combined, 2 to 3 minutes. Add the eggs, one at a time, beating after each one to blend it into the butter mixture. Stir the jam well, add it to the batter, and beat at low speed to mix it in.

ADD THE FLOUR and stir well with a wooden spoon or a spatula, incorporating it into the batter. Add the milk and continue stirring only until the milk disappears.

QUICKLY SCRAPE THE BATTER into the pans and bake at 350°F for 25 to 30 minutes, until the cakes are nicely browned, spring back when touched gently in the center, and are beginning to pull away from the sides of the pans.

COOL THE CAKES in the pans on wire racks or folded kitchen towels for 10 minutes, and then turn out the cakes onto wire racks or plates to cool completely, top side up.

Caramel Glaze

- ½ cup (1 stick) butter
- 1 cup light brown sugar
- ½ cup evaporated milk or half-and-half
- One 1-pound box (about 3⅔ cups) confectioners' sugar, sifted
- 1 teaspoon vanilla extract

TO MAKE THE GLAZE, combine the butter and sugar in a medium saucepan. Stir over medium heat until the butter melts and blends with the sugar into a smooth sauce, 2 to 3 minutes. Add the milk, and let the icing come to a gentle boil. Stir well, remove from the heat, and add the sifted confectioners' sugar and the vanilla. Beat well with a mixer, whisk, or spoon for 1 or 2 minutes, until the icing thickens and loses a little of its shine. Use at once. If the glaze hardens, stir in 1 or 2 spoonfuls of evaporated milk to soften it.

TO COMPLETE THE CAKE, place one layer, top side down, on a cake stand or serving plate, and spread it generously with the glaze. Place the second layer over the first, top side down, and ice it. (If you've baked only 2 layers, place the second layer top side up.) Add the third layer, top side up, and pour the remaining icing over its surface, spreading it to cover the top and then encouraging any extra icing to drip invitingly down the uniced sides of the cake.

Enjoy this simple, delicious cake for breakfast, a tea party, or a midnight snack. If you can't pick your own blueberries in the Shenandoah Valley, don't worry. The cake comes out just fine using fresh blueberries from wherever you are, or even frozen berries in the middle of winter. The recipe is from *The Best of the Bushel*, a delicious volume of recipes from the Junior League of Charlottesville, Virginia.

Shenandoah Valley Blueberry Cake

SERVES 6 TO 8

- 1⅔ cups all-purpose flour
- 1½ teaspoons baking powder
- ¼ teaspoon salt
- ⅓ cup butter, softened
- ¾ cup plus 2 tablespoons sugar
- 1 egg
- ⅓ cup milk
- 1 cup fresh or frozen blueberries (do not thaw)

HEAT THE OVEN to 375°F, and generously grease a 9-inch square or round pan.

COMBINE the flour, baking powder, and salt in a small bowl, and stir with a fork to mix well. In a medium bowl, combine the butter and sugar, and beat with a mixer at high speed until well combined. Add the egg and beat well for 1 to 2 minutes, stopping to scrape down the bowl, until the mixture is smooth and light.

STIR IN HALF THE FLOUR MIXTURE, then half the milk, mixing just enough to keep the batter fairly smooth and well combined. Add the remaining flour, then the rest of the milk, mixing gently. Stir in the blueberries.

SCRAPE THE BATTER into the prepared pan, and bake at 375°F for 30 minutes, or until the cake is golden, springs back when touched gently in the center, and is pulling away from the sides of the pan.

SERVE A SQUARE CAKE right from the pan, warm or at room temperature, cut into small squares. If it's round, let the cake cool in the pan on a wire rack or folded kitchen towel for 10 minutes, and then turn it out to cool on a wire rack, top side up.

No, Hawaii is not a Southern state, even by the most creative geographical thinking. But since the Dole company put canned pineapple on the map early in the last century, this cake has been a standard contribution to Southern covered-dish suppers, family reunions, church homecomings, and dinners on the grounds. A Dole company recipe contest held in 1924 received more than 2,000 entries for pineapple upside-down cake, a sure sign that the upside-down cake idea had been around a good while, and that the pineapple rings and brown sugar combination was a keeper. Originally made in a cast-iron skillet, the cake works nicely in round or square cake pans.

Pineapple Upside-Down Cake

SERVES 6 TO 8

HEAT THE OVEN to 350°F.

TO MAKE THE TOPPING, drain the pineapple well, reserving 2 tablespoons of the juice or syrup for the cake batter. Melt the cold butter in a 10-inch cast-iron skillet over medium heat. Or put the butter in a 9-inch round cake pan and put it in the oven for a few minutes as it heats to melt the butter. Remove the pan from the oven or stove, and sprinkle the brown sugar over its buttery surface. Place the pineapple rings carefully on top of the scattered brown sugar and melted butter, arranging them so they fit in 1 layer. (You may have a few left over.) Place a cherry in the center of each ring, and set the pan aside.

TO MAKE THE CAKE, in a large mixing bowl, combine the flour, sugar, baking powder, and salt, and use a fork to mix them together well. Add the milk and butter, and beat well with a mixer at medium speed, scraping down the bowl once or twice, until you have a thick, fairly smooth batter, 1 to 2 minutes. Add the egg, reserved pineapple syrup or juice, and the vanilla. Beat for 2 minutes more, stopping once or twice to scrape down the bowl.

CAREFULLY POUR THE BATTER over the pineapple arranged in the skillet or cake pan, and use a spoon or a spatula to spread it evenly to the edges of the pan. Bake at 350°F for 35 to 40 minutes, until the cake is golden brown and springs back when touched lightly in the center. Cool in the skillet or pan for 5 minutes on a wire rack or a folded kitchen towel. With oven mitts, carefully turn out the warm cake onto a serving plate by placing the plate upside down over the cake in the skillet, and then flipping them over together to release the cake onto the plate. Serve warm, or cool to room temperature before serving.

Pineapple Topping

- One 20-ounce can pineapple rings, with their syrup or juice
- 4 tablespoons cold butter
- 2/3 cup firmly packed brown sugar, light or dark
- 10 maraschino cherries

Cake

- 1½ cups all-purpose flour
- ¾ cup sugar
- 1½ teaspoons baking powder
- ½ teaspoon salt
- ½ cup milk
- 4 tablespoons butter, softened
- 1 egg
- 1 teaspoon vanilla extract

My mother made this cake each autumn, because we loved it and because it is the ultimate good traveler. Baked in a 13-by-9-inch pan, it yields a big, dense, and delicious rectangle of apples, nuts, and caramel-kissed glaze, one which won't budge from its foil-covered pan until you are good and ready to cut it. It's perfect for school lunches, leaf-viewing hikes, tailgate picnics, and potluck suppers. Like carrot cake, it calls for oil rather than butter, and requires only a quick stir to get it into the oven. You could also bake this cake in a tube or Bundt pan; add some cinnamon and nutmeg and make it more of an apple pound cake.

Fresh Apple Cake *with Brown Sugar Glaze*

SERVES 8 TO 10

Fresh Apple Cake

- 3 cups all-purpose flour
- 2 cups sugar
- 1 teaspoon baking soda
- 1 teaspoon salt
- 3 eggs
- 1½ cups vegetable oil
- 2 teaspoons vanilla extract
- 3 cups finely chopped apples
- 1 cup coarsely chopped pecans or walnuts

Brown Sugar Glaze

- 1 cup lightly packed light brown sugar
- ⅓ cup butter
- 1 teaspoon vanilla extract
- 2 tablespoons evaporated milk, half-and-half, or cream

TO MAKE THE CAKE, heat the oven to 350°F. Grease a 13-by-9-inch pan, or two 8- or 9-inch cake pans, round or square. In a medium bowl, combine the flour, sugar, baking soda, and salt, and stir with a fork to mix everything together well.

IN A LARGE BOWL, beat the eggs with a wooden spoon or a mixer at low speed until pale yellow and foamy. Add the oil and vanilla, and beat well. Stir in the flour mixture with a wooden spoon and continue stirring the batter just until the flour disappears. Add the apples and nuts, stir to mix them into the batter until fairly uniform, and scrape the batter into the prepared pans.

BAKE at 350°F for 45 to 50 minutes, or until the cake is golden brown, springs back when touched lightly near the center, and is beginning to pull away from the sides of the pan. Place the cake on a wire rack or a folded kitchen towel.

MAKE THE GLAZE while the cake is hot. Combine all the ingredients in a medium saucepan. Cook over medium heat, stirring often, until the mixture comes to a gentle boil, and cook for 3 to 5 minutes.

SPOON THE GLAZE all over the hot-from-the-oven cake. Let the glazed cake cool completely, and serve in squares right from the pan.

Stack cake is an Appalachian mountain original, a sturdy, homespun tower of thin gingerbread layers, fortified with sorghum or molasses, enlivened with sweet spices, and held steady by a delicious dried apple-spice puree. My friend Dean's Aunt Lou was the stack cake queen of Alleghany County, North Carolina, renowned for her molasses-laced, six-layer versions. You'll find believers in dough instead of batter, rolled dough instead of patted, stovetop versus oven, and sweetening with sorghum, not molasses. My batter version takes a little time and a number of steps, but each part is simple and the resulting cake is a memorable homespun treat.

Alleghany County Molasses Stack Cake

SERVES 6 TO 8

Spice Cake Layers

- 4 cups all-purpose flour
- 2 teaspoons baking powder
- ½ teaspoon baking soda
- ½ teaspoon salt
- 2 teaspoons ground ginger
- 1 teaspoon ground cinnamon
- ½ teaspoon ground nutmeg
- ½ teaspoon ground allspice
- ¼ teaspoon ground cloves
- 1 cup buttermilk (see Note) or milk
- 3 eggs, beaten well
- 1 cup (2 sticks) butter, softened, or 1 cup shortening
- 1 cup brown sugar, light or dark
- 1 cup molasses or sorghum

TO MAKE THE CAKE, heat the oven to 350°F. Grease two or more 9-inch round cake pans generously. You'll be making a total of 6 thin layers, so prepare as many pans as you have, or plan to bake in several shifts if need be. In a large bowl, combine the flour, baking powder, baking soda, salt, and all the spices. Sift together, or use a fork to combine all the dry ingredients well. Stir the milk into the eggs in a medium bowl and beat well.

COMBINE the butter, sugar, and molasses in a large bowl, and beat with a mixer at high speed to blend them together well. Add about one third of the flour mixture, beating at low speed until it disappears into the batter. Then add half the egg mixture, beating just until it is mixed in. Add another third of the flour, then the rest of the egg mixture, and then the last of the flour, beating each time only enough to smooth out the batter.

POUR 1 CUP OF THE BATTER into each of the prepared pans, and tip the pan to spread it out to the edges. Bake at 350°F for 10 to 12 minutes, until the cakes spring back when touched lightly in the center and are beginning to pull away from the sides of the pans. Cool in the pans on wire racks or folded kitchen towels for 10 minutes. Then carefully transfer the very thin cakes to the wire racks or plates to cool completely, top side up. Continue until you have baked all the batter into 6 thin, spice-infused cakes.

TO MAKE THE FILLING, chop the apples coarsely, and place them in a large bowl or pan with the warm water or apple cider. Set aside for 3 hours, or as long as overnight. Remove apples and chop coarsely. Place in a large saucepan along with the soaking liquid. Place over medium heat, and bring to a gentle boil, stirring now and then. Add more

Dried Apple Spice Filling

- 1 pound dried apples (about 4 cups)
- 4 to 6 cups warm water or warm apple cider
- 1 cup brown sugar, light or dark
- 1 teaspoon ground cinnamon
- 1 teaspoon ground nutmeg
- 1 teaspoon ground ginger
- ½ teaspoon ground allspice
- ¼ teaspoon ground cloves
- ¼ teaspoon salt

liquid if needed. Reduce the heat to maintain a gentle but lively simmer. Cook for 20 to 25 minutes, stirring now and then, until the apples are soft and the liquid has cooked away. Remove from the heat, stir in the brown sugar, cinnamon, nutmeg, ginger, allspice, cloves, and salt, and mash to a fairly smooth sauce. Cool to room temperature.

TO COMPLETE THE CAKE, place one layer, top side up, on a cake stand or serving platter, saving the most beautiful layer for the top of the cake. Spoon about one fifth of the apple filling on the cake, and spread it out evenly all the way to the edges. Continue filling and stacking the layers, top side up, finishing with one plain layer on top. Set the cake aside to season for at least 3 hours and as long as 1 day. Then serve, or cover tightly and refrigerate for up to 2 days more. You can dust the top of the cake with confectioners' sugar shortly before serving, and offer sweetened whipped cream on the side if you like.

NOTE: If you don't have buttermilk, stir 1 tablespoon of vinegar or lemon juice into 1 cup of milk and let stand for 10 minutes.

CHOCOLATE CAKES, SOUTHERN STYLE

Southerners don't think of chocolate as particularly Southern; they just love having it as an option when creating divine sweets and desserts. Cocoa is most common in the modern Southern kitchen, but unsweetened and bittersweet chocolate played a bigger role in the Southern kitchens of the eighteenth and much of the nineteenth centuries. Older recipes often call for chocolate to be grated, and measurements are given in weights, as were all ingredients for baking at the time.

SYBIL PRESSLY'S BUTTERMILK CAKE WITH OLD-TIME FUDGE ICING (page 132) would have been called a chocolate layer cake in olden days, even though the layers are yellow. That was when chocolate icing was newfangled and grand, and chocolate enough to earn the name. Now "chocolate layer cake" conjures up a vision of dark, chocolatey layers and a frosting to match. CHOCOLATE MAYONNAISE CAKE WITH DIVINITY ICING (page 134), another classic, combines deep, moist chocolate flavor with a heavenly cloud of vanilla frosting.

Make CHOCOLATE WET CAKE WITH SPEEDY CHOCOLATE FROSTING (page 141) or MISSISSIPPI MUD CAKE (page 137) whenever you want a quick but fabulous chocolate cake for a casual celebration. Let JACKIE BAYS' WHITE CHOCOLATE LAYER CAKE (page 142) provide ethereal elegance for a special birthday celebration. When your table needs a dazzling centerpiece with minimal fuss, bake HELEN HUDSON WHITING'S CELESTIAL CHOCOLATE CAKE (page 138), a gorgeous cake worthy of any occasion.

During her years as innkeeper and executive chef of the historic Mast Farm Inn in the Blue Ridge Mountains of North Carolina, Sybil Pressly put her mother's chocolate-frosted buttermilk layer cake on the menu and never took it off. Comforting and somehow familiar, even when you taste it for the first time, this cake belongs in your recipe box, whether it's extensive or just a folder on the bookshelf. Mrs. Pressly uses these same yellow layers for her famous pineapple cream cake and her shortcake. The cake has never let her down, but she warns all cooks that this heirloom chocolate icing simply will not work on a rainy day.

Sybil Pressly's Buttermilk Cake with Old-Time Fudge Icing

SERVES 6 TO 8

TO MAKE THE CAKE, heat the oven to 375°F. Grease and flour three 8-inch round cake pans. In a medium bowl, combine the flour, baking powder, salt, and baking soda, and stir with a fork to mix well.

IN A LARGE BOWL, combine the softened butter and the sugar, and beat with a mixer at high speed until very light, fluffy, and smooth, 6 to 8 minutes. Add the eggs, one at a time, beating well after each one.

ADD ABOUT A THIRD of the flour mixture, and then half the milk, beating at low speed just until the flour or the milk disappears. Mix in another third of the flour, followed by the rest of the milk, and then the rest of the flour in the same way. Stir in the vanilla, and divide the batter among the 3 prepared cake pans.

BAKE at 375°F for 20 to 25 minutes, until the cakes are golden brown and spring back when touched lightly in the center. Cool the cakes in the pans on wire racks or on folded kitchen towels for 10 minutes. Then turn out the cakes onto wire racks or plates, top side up, to cool completely.

TO MAKE THE FROSTING, first place a bowl of ice water and a metal spoon by the stove. Place one cake layer, top side down, on a cake stand or serving plate. Have the other two layers handy so that you can ice the cake as soon as the icing is ready.

BREAK THE CHOCOLATE SQUARES into big chunks, and then combine them in a medium heavy saucepan with the brown sugar, corn syrup, salt, and evaporated milk. Bring everything to a boil over medium heat, stirring often to help melt the chocolate and prevent it from sticking and burning. Continue cooking the icing at a gentle boil, until it reaches the soft-ball stage. This means that a generous dollop of the icing dropped into cold water forms a soft little clump, which

Buttermilk Cake

- 3 cups all-purpose flour
- 2 teaspoons baking powder
- ½ teaspoon salt
- ½ teaspoon baking soda
- 1 cup (2 sticks) butter, softened
- 2 cups sugar
- 4 eggs
- 1 cup buttermilk (see Note)
- 1 teaspoon vanilla extract

Pressly's Old-Time Fudge Icing

Three 1-ounce squares unsweetened chocolate, or ½ cup cocoa

3 cups light brown sugar

2 tablespoons light corn syrup

⅛ teaspoon salt

1 cup evaporated milk or half-and-half

2 tablespoons butter

1 teaspoon vanilla extract

can be rolled between your fingers into a tiny ball. The temperature on a candy thermometer will read 236 to 240°F.

REMOVE THE PAN from the heat. Without stirring, add the butter and vanilla to the pan on top of the icing, and let the frosting cool to lukewarm. Then, mix it at medium speed until it loses its shine and thickens enough to spread on the cake.

QUICKLY COVER the first cake layer with icing, and place the second layer on top of it, top side down. Cover it with icing, and then place the third layer over the second, top side up. Pour the icing over the cake and quickly spread it over the sides and top. If the icing hardens while you are working, add a little milk and stir well to soften it again.

NOTE: If you don't have buttermilk, stir 1 tablespoon of vinegar or lemon juice into 1 cup of milk and let stand for 10 minutes.

This simple, moist cake with the "beg your pardon?" ingredient makes a grand companion for sweet, fluffy white icing. A popular pairing in the first half of the twentieth century, this combination of dark chocolate cake with sweet white icing faded away as cooked frostings moved to the back burner and quick confectioners' sugar frostings tap-danced out to center stage.

Chocolate Mayonnaise Cake *with Divinity Icing*

SERVES 6 TO 8

The use of mayonnaise in a cake probably began as an economy measure. Its ready-made mixture of eggs and oil offered a kitchen shortcut, and a way to save money on two costly ingredients: butter and eggs. I love this cake's deep chocolate color and flavor, and its moist, delicate texture. Because it's a bit fragile, I always line the cake pans with waxed paper or kitchen parchment before baking, and let the layers cool completely in the pans before turning them out with great care.

Chocolate Mayonnaise Cake

- ½ cup cocoa
- 1 cup boiling water
- 2 cups all-purpose flour
- 1 cup sugar
- 2 teaspoons baking soda
- ½ teaspoon salt
- 1 cup mayonnaise
- 1 teaspoon vanilla extract

TO MAKE THE CAKE, heat the oven to 350°F. Grease two 8-inch or 9-inch round cake pans generously, line the bottom of each pan with a circle of waxed paper or kitchen parchment, grease the paper, and flour the pan. Measure the cocoa into a medium bowl, and add the boiling water, stirring with a whisk or a fork to mix them together well. Set aside to cool. Combine the flour, sugar, baking soda, and salt in a medium bowl, and stir with a fork to mix everything together well.

WHEN THE COCOA MIXTURE has cooled, add the mayonnaise and vanilla, and stir with a wooden spoon, spatula, or whisk to combine everything well. Gently sprinkle the flour mixture onto the batter, and then beat until the batter is smooth and thin. Quickly divide the batter among the pans.

BAKE at 350°F for 25 to 30 minutes, until the cakes spring back when touched gently in the center and are beginning to pull away from the sides of the pans. Cool completely in the pans on wire racks or folded kitchen towels.

TO MAKE THE FROSTING, bring about 3 inches of water to an active simmer in the bottom of a double boiler or a medium saucepan. Meanwhile, in the top of the double boiler, or in a heat-proof bowl that

Old-Fashioned Divinity Icing

- 1 cup sugar
- ¼ cup light corn syrup
- ¼ cup water
- 2 egg whites
- ¼ teaspoon salt
- ¼ teaspoon cream of tartar
- 1 teaspoon vanilla extract

will sit snugly over the saucepan, combine the sugar, corn syrup, water, egg whites, salt, and cream of tartar. Beat with a mixer at low speed for 1 minute, until the mixture is pale yellow and very foamy. Place the pan or bowl of icing over the simmering water, and beat at high speed for 7 minutes or more, until the icing becomes white, thick, and shiny and triples in volume. Continue beating until the icing forms firm peaks and loses some of its shine. (This whole process could take as long as 15 to 20 minutes.) Remove the icing from the heat, add the vanilla, and continue beating for 2 minutes more.

TO COMPLETE THE CAKE, very carefully invert each cooled cake layer onto a wire rack or a plate, and remove the waxed paper. Place one layer on a cake stand or serving plate, top side down, and frost it generously with about one third of the icing. Cover with the second layer, and generously frost the sides and then the top of the cake.

Southerners love this earthy cake—the way it looks, the way it tastes, and especially its wacky name. You don't have to be from Mississippi—or even Southern—to come under its spell. The main requirement, judging from the response during a help-us-eat-all-these-cakes party we hosted a while back, is that you be in the room with it and be able to reach the cake plate. How its components transform themselves into such a tasty cake is a mystery to me, since it's ready for the oven after only two simple steps.

Mississippi Mud Cake

SERVES 10 TO 12

Cake

- 1 cup (2 sticks) butter, cut into big chunks
- ½ cup cocoa
- 4 eggs, beaten well
- 1 teaspoon vanilla extract
- 2 cups sugar
- 1½ cups all-purpose flour
- ⅛ teaspoon salt
- 1 cup chopped pecans or walnuts

Mississippi Mud Frosting

- One 16-ounce box (about 3⅔ cups) confectioners' sugar
- ½ cup cocoa
- ½ cup (1 stick) butter, melted
- ½ cup milk or evaporated milk
- 1 teaspoon vanilla extract
- 4 cups mini-marshmallows, or 3 cups marshmallows, quartered

TO MAKE THE CAKE, heat the oven to 350°F. Grease and flour a 13-by-9-inch pan. In a medium saucepan, combine the butter and the cocoa and cook over medium heat, stirring now and then, until the butter is melted and the mixture is well blended, 3 to 4 minutes. Stir in the beaten eggs, vanilla, sugar, flour, salt, and pecans, and beat with a wooden spoon or a spatula or with a mixer at low speed until the batter is well combined and smooth, and the flour has disappeared.

QUICKLY POUR THE BATTER into the prepared pan and bake at 350°F for 20 to 25 minutes, until the cake springs back when touched gently in the center and is beginning to pull away from the sides of the pan.

PREPARE THE FROSTING while the cake bakes, so that you will be ready to pour it over the hot cake. In a medium bowl, combine the confectioners' sugar and the cocoa, and stir to mix them well. Add the melted butter, milk, and vanilla, and use a large spoon or a mixer at low speed to beat everything together well. Set aside until the cake is done.

REMOVE THE CAKE from the oven, scatter the marshmallows over the top, and return the cake to the hot oven for about 3 minutes, to soften the marshmallows.

PLACE THE CAKE, still in the pan, on a wire rack or a folded kitchen towel. Pour the frosting all over the marshmallow-dotted cake, and cool to room temperature. Cut into small squares and serve.

This recipe comes from a jewel of a book called *In Helen's Kitchen: A Philosophy of Food.* Published in memory of Helen Hudson Whiting by her friends at the Regulator Bookstore in Durham, North Carolina, in 2000, the book includes many of her eloquent and witty food columns and recipes, written for area publications through the 1970s and '80s. It also contains an abundance of keepsake recipes shared by Helen's family and friends. This cake, a family favorite for birthdays, came from Helen's mother, and it makes a heavenly and elegant celebration cake.

Helen Hudson Whiting's Celestial Chocolate Cake

SERVES 8 TO 10

TO MAKE THE CAKE, heat the oven to 350°F, and grease and flour three 9-inch round cake pans.

POUR THE BOILING WATER over the cocoa. Stir well with a fork until smooth, and set aside to cool. Combine the flour, baking soda, baking powder, and salt in a medium bowl, and stir with a fork to mix well.

COMBINE the butter and sugar in a large bowl, and beat with a mixer at high speed until well combined. Add the vanilla and then the eggs, one at a time, beating well after each one until the mixture is smooth and light. Add the flour mixture in 4 batches, beating after each addition only until the flour disappears. Add the cocoa mixture in 3 batches, beating just enough after each addition to combine everything into a smooth, luscious batter, stopping once or twice to scrape down the sides of the bowl.

DIVIDE THE BATTER among the 3 cake pans. Bake at 350°F for 25 to 30 minutes, until the cakes spring back when touched lightly in the center and are beginning to pull away from the sides of the pans.

COOL THE CAKES for 10 minutes in the pans on wire racks or folded kitchen towels. Then gently turn them out onto wire racks or plates to cool completely, top side up.

TO MAKE THE FILLING, in a medium bowl, combine the whipping cream, confectioners' sugar, and vanilla, and beat until thick and luscious. Cover and refrigerate until you are ready to complete the cake.

TO MAKE THE FROSTING, in a medium saucepan, combine the chocolate chips, cream, and butter. Cook gently over medium heat, stirring often to help the butter and chocolate melt, and to avoid letting the mixture come to a boil. When the chocolate and butter have melted, transfer the mixture

Helen's Celestial Cake

- 2 cups boiling water
- 1 cup cocoa
- 2¾ cups all-purpose flour
- 2 teaspoons baking soda
- ½ teaspoon baking powder
- ½ teaspoon salt
- 1 cup (2 sticks) butter
- 2½ cups sugar
- ½ teaspoon vanilla extract
- 4 eggs

Cream Filling

- 1 cup very cold heavy cream or whipping cream
- ¼ cup confectioners' sugar
- 1 teaspoon vanilla extract

CONTINUED

CONTINUED

to a medium bowl, and let cool to room temperature. Add the confectioners' sugar and beat well with a mixer at medium speed until thick enough to spread, stopping often to scrape down the bowl.

TO COMPLETE THE CAKE, place the first layer, top side down, on a cake or serving plate, and spread half the whipped cream filling almost to the edge. Cover with a second layer, top side down, and spread the remaining whipped cream filling almost to the edge. Place the third layer, top side up, over the filling. Spread the chocolate frosting over the sides and then the top of the cake.

Helen's Chocolate Frosting

One 16-ounce package semisweet chocolate chips (about 2¾ cups)

½ cup heavy cream or whipping cream

1 cup (2 sticks) butter, cut into chunks

2½ cups confectioners' sugar

This dandy little cake may not have been born in the South, but it was lovingly adopted by Southerners who have an affection for delicious, quirky, and unusual cakes. It isn't really wet, but the texture is unique, somewhere between fudge, cake, and a milk chocolate candy bar. No need for the mixer here; a wooden spoon, fork, whisk, or eggbeater is the low-tech way to go. When you want a make-it-fast or take-it-with-you cake, this one is a sweet, sure thing. Enjoy it in small squares like a brownie, or cut it into larger squares and serve it on dessert plates.

Chocolate Wet Cake *with Speedy Chocolate Frosting*

SERVES 10 TO 12

TO MAKE THE CAKE, heat the oven to 400°F, and grease a 13-by-9-inch baking pan generously. Combine the cocoa, water, and butter or shortening in a medium saucepan, and place it on the stove over medium heat. Stir now and then, helping the butter melt and mixing everything together into a smooth chocolate sauce. As soon as it comes to a gentle boil, remove the pan from the heat and set aside to cool.

IN A LARGE BOWL, combine the flour, sugar, cinnamon, baking soda, and salt, and stir them together with a fork. In a medium bowl, combine the buttermilk, eggs, and vanilla, and stir with a fork to mix them well.

COMBINE all three mixtures, pouring both the chocolate and the egg mixtures over the flour in the big bowl. Use a big wooden spoon or a spatula to stir everything together into a smooth chocolate batter. Pour the batter into the prepared pan.

BAKE at 400°F for 25 minutes, until the cake is firm and shiny and springs back when touched lightly in the center. Cool the cake in the pan on a wire rack or folded kitchen towel.

TO MAKE THE FROSTING, in a medium saucepan, combine the butter, cocoa or chocolate, and milk, and place over medium heat. Stir now and then, nudging the butter to melt and blending the ingredients into a smooth, chocolatey sauce. Remove from the heat and add the confectioners' sugar and vanilla to the pan. Using a wooden spoon, beat the mixture until the confectioners' sugar disappears and the frosting reaches a medium-thick, spreadable consistency.

SPREAD THE FROSTING over the cooled cake. Let it stand for 30 minutes before cutting the cake into small squares.

NOTE: If you don't have buttermilk, stir 1½ teaspoons of vinegar or lemon juice into ½ cup of milk, and let stand for 10 minutes.

Chocolate Wet Cake

¼ cup cocoa

1 cup water

1 cup (2 sticks) butter, cut into 6 chunks; or 1 cup shortening

2 cups all-purpose flour

2 cups sugar

1 teaspoon ground cinnamon

1 teaspoon baking soda

¼ teaspoon salt

½ cup buttermilk (see Note)

2 eggs

1 teaspoon vanilla extract

Speedy Chocolate Frosting

½ cup (1 stick) butter, cut into 6 chunks

2 tablespoons cocoa, or one 1-ounce square unsweetened chocolate

3 tablespoons evaporated milk, half-and-half, or milk

About 3 cups confectioners' sugar

½ teaspoon vanilla extract

White chocolate is sweet as can be and luxurious in texture, providing a delicate whisper of a chocolate presence that is easy to love. This recipe from Jackie Bays of Jackson, Kentucky, creates a home-style buttermilk cake with a heavenly note of white chocolate. If possible, refrigerate the cake for an hour or more before serving.

Jackie Bays' White Chocolate Layer Cake

SERVES 8 TO 10

TO MAKE THE CAKE, heat the oven to 350°F, and grease three 8-inch round cake pans or two 9-inch round cake pans; line the bottom of each pan with a circle of waxed paper or kitchen parchment and flour the pan.

COMBINE the flour, baking soda, and salt in a medium bowl, and stir with a fork to mix them well.

BRING ABOUT 3 INCHES OF WATER to an active simmer in the bottom of a double boiler or a saucepan that will accommodate a medium heat-proof bowl so that it sits snugly over the water. Melt the white chocolate in the top of the double boiler or in the bowl over the simmering water. Stir often, and then pour in the ½ cup of boiling water and stir to mix well. Remove from the heat.

IN A MEDIUM BOWL, combine the butter and sugar and beat with a mixer at medium speed to mix them together well. Add the egg yolks, one by one, beating each time to keep the mixture smooth. Add the white chocolate and the vanilla, and stir to mix well.

ADD ABOUT A THIRD of the flour mixture, and then about half of the buttermilk, beating with a mixer at low speed just long enough, after each addition, to make the flour or the buttermilk disappear into the batter. Mix in another third of the flour, the remaining buttermilk, and then the last of the flour in the same way.

IN A MEDIUM BOWL, beat the egg whites at medium speed until they are foamy and opaque. Continue beating at high speed until they swell into thick, pillowy mounds and hold peaks that are stiff but not dry. Add about one third of the egg white mixture to the bowl of batter, and fold it in gently using your spatula. Add the remaining egg whites and continue folding with a light touch, until the egg whites are blended in well, with only a few streaks showing.

White Chocolate Cake

- 2½ cups sifted cake flour
- 1 teaspoon baking soda
- ½ teaspoon salt
- 4 ounces white chocolate, finely chopped
- ½ cup boiling water
- 1 cup (2 sticks) butter, softened
- 2 cups sugar
- 4 eggs, separated
- 1 teaspoon vanilla extract
- 1 cup buttermilk (see Note)

White Chocolate Frosting

- 6 ounces white chocolate, finely chopped
- 12 ounces cream cheese (1½ cups), softened
- 3 tablespoons butter, softened
- ¾ teaspoon vanilla extract
- 3 cups confectioners' sugar

TRANSFER THE BATTER to the prepared pans and bake at 350°F for 25 to 30 minutes, until the cakes are golden brown, spring back when touched gently in the center, and are beginning to pull away from the sides of the pans.

COOL THE CAKES in the pans on wire racks or folded kitchen towels for about 30 minutes. Turn them out onto wire racks or plates, peel off the paper, and turn them right side up to cool completely.

PREPARE THE FROSTING while the cakes are cooling. In the top of the double boiler or in the heatproof bowl, melt the white chocolate over hot, not simmering, water, stirring often. Remove from the heat and let cool to lukewarm. Transfer the melted white chocolate to a large bowl, and add the cream cheese, butter, and vanilla. Beat together at medium speed until you have a smooth sauce. Add the confectioners' sugar, and beat until smooth, well mixed, and just right for spreading on the cake.

TO COMPLETE THE CAKE, place one layer, top side down, on a cake stand or serving plate, and spread it with about one fourth of the icing for a 3-layer cake, and about one third for a 2-layer cake. Continue stacking and frosting the layers. The uppermost layer should sit top side up. Cover the sides and then the top with the remaining frosting.

COVER THE CAKE and refrigerate for at least 1 hour. Set the cake out about 30 minutes before serving time.

NOTE: If you don't have buttermilk, stir 1 tablespoon of vinegar or lemon juice into 1 cup of milk, and let stand for 10 minutes.

FROSTINGS, ICINGS, AND FILLINGS

Here you'll find an assortment of wonderful frostings. Some are old-timey and involve cooking sugar and butter into a fudgy, delicious icing. Others are as easy as beating confectioners' sugar with butter and vanilla to make a sweet, simple finish for an everyday cake.

The chapter ends with several recipes that utilize classic cooking techniques, none of them beyond the scope of home cooks. LEMON CURD (page 157) is fabulous, both as a cake filling and as a treat with pound cake, scones, or an English tea. BOILED CUSTARD (page 158) is a Christmas tradition in Kentucky and is a central element of tipsy cake, a Southern take on English trifles.

Pair these frostings with cakes and cake layers from any chapter in this book. The idea is to enjoy baking and sharing your creations with people you care about. Learn the basics and then you can strike out on your own, as good cooks have always done, in the South and around the world.

Making this frosting is so easy that you will soon be mixing up your favorite flavors without even looking at the recipe. Make vanilla first. Next try your hand at a variation or two; then start concocting frostings to complement the cakes you want to make.

Everyday Confectioners' Sugar Frosting

MAKES ENOUGH FOR ONE 3-LAYER CAKE, ONE 13-BY-9-INCH CAKE, OR 24 CUPCAKES

- ½ cup (1 stick) butter, softened
- One 1-pound box (3⅔ cups) confectioners' sugar
- 1 teaspoon vanilla extract
- ¼ teaspoon salt
- 2 tablespoons milk, half-and-half, or evaporated milk

IN A MEDIUM BOWL, beat the butter with a mixer at medium speed until creamy and smooth. Add the confectioners' sugar, vanilla, and salt, and beat for 1 minute. Add the milk and beat well at high speed, stopping often to scrape down the bowl, until the frosting is smooth and creamy and a nice texture for spreading on your cake.

VARIATIONS

Chocolate Frosting

Replace ½ cup of the confectioners' sugar with ⅔ cup of cocoa before you begin mixing the frosting.

Strawberry, Blackberry, or Raspberry Frosting

Increase the confectioners' sugar by ⅓ cup, and add ⅓ cup of jam (strawberry, blackberry, or raspberry) along with the milk.

Lemon or Orange Frosting

Omit the vanilla, and substitute 1 teaspoon of lemon extract and 2 teaspoons of grated lemon zest, or 1 teaspoon of orange extract and 2 teaspoons of grated orange zest. Or beat in 3 tablespoons of **Lemon Curd** (page 157) along with the milk, again omitting the vanilla.

Keep in mind that the "seven-minute" title expresses a rather idealistic goal. In fact, this sweet, cloudlike frosting may take as long as 20 minutes to reach its proper shiny and voluptuous state. It will be gorgeous, and worth every minute.

Seven-Minute Frosting

MAKES ENOUGH FOR ANY LAYER CAKE, TWO 13-BY-9-INCH CAKES, OR 3 TO 4 DOZEN CUPCAKES

1 cup sugar
¼ cup light corn syrup
¼ cup water
2 egg whites
¼ teaspoon salt
¼ teaspoon cream of tartar
1 teaspoon vanilla extract

BRING ABOUT 3 INCHES OF WATER to an active simmer in the bottom of a double boiler or a medium saucepan. Meanwhile, in the top of the double boiler or in a heat-proof bowl that will fit snugly over the saucepan, combine the sugar, corn syrup, water, egg whites, salt, and cream of tartar. Beat with a mixer at low speed for 1 minute, until the mixture is pale yellow and very foamy.

PLACE THE PAN OR BOWL OF ICING over the simmering water, and beat at high speed for 7 to 14 minutes or more, until the frosting becomes white, thick, and shiny, and triples in volume. Continue beating until the frosting forms firm peaks and loses some of its shine. Remove the frosting from the heat, add the vanilla, and continue beating for 2 minutes more. Spread quickly on the cake layers.

This is the classic companion to carrot cake (see pages 100 and 118), and it is often paired with **Red Velvet Cake** (page 103) as well. Delicious and easy to prepare, cream cheese frosting makes a fine complement to any rich, flavorful cake.

Cream Cheese Frosting

MAKES ENOUGH FOR ONE 3-LAYER CAKE, ONE 13-BY-9-INCH CAKE, OR 24 CUPCAKES

One 8-ounce package cream cheese, softened (1 cup)

¼ cup (½ stick) butter, softened

One 1-pound box (3⅔ cups) confectioners' sugar, sifted

1 teaspoon vanilla extract

IN A MEDIUM BOWL, combine the cream cheese and butter and beat with a mixer on medium speed to mix well. Add the confectioners' sugar and vanilla and beat at high speed until the frosting is fluffy and smooth, stopping once or twice to scrape down the bowl and mix everything well. Spread the frosting on a cooled cake, or cover and refrigerate for up to 3 days.

The simple step of melting butter to a warm brown color and toasty flavor makes for a delicious and handsome frosting. Try this with chocolate cake or banana cake, as well as a standard yellow cake.

Browned Butter Frosting

MAKES ENOUGH FOR ONE 3-LAYER CAKE, ONE 13-BY-9-INCH CAKE, OR 24 CUPCAKES

6 tablespoons butter

3 cups confectioners' sugar, sifted

1½ teaspoons vanilla extract

3 to 4 tablespoons milk, half-and-half, or evaporated milk

MELT THE BUTTER in a small saucepan over medium heat, swirling the pan and stirring almost constantly. The butter should foam and bubble, and turn a lovely golden brown, but not burn. Remove from the heat and set aside to cool to room temperature.

TO FINISH THE FROSTING, combine the browned butter with the confectioners' sugar and vanilla in a medium bowl. Beat with a mixer at medium speed to blend the ingredients, scraping down the bowl now and then. Add 2 tablespoons of the milk, and continue beating until the frosting is smooth. Add more milk, a bit at a time, as needed, until the frosting is a spreadable consistency.

This simple, old-fashioned frosting sets up like fudge and is simple to make. I love this on yellow and white layers for contrast, and on chocolate layers for deep chocolate pleasure.

Old-Fashioned Chocolate Fudge Frosting

MAKES ENOUGH FOR ONE 2-LAYER CAKE OR ONE 13-BY-9-INCH CAKE

- 1½ cups sugar
- ¼ cup cocoa
- ¼ teaspoon salt
- ¼ cup (½ stick) butter
- ½ cup evaporated milk or half-and-half
- 1 teaspoon vanilla extract

IN A HEAVY MEDIUM SAUCEPAN, combine the sugar, cocoa, and salt, and stir or whisk to mix everything well. Add the butter and the milk and place over medium heat, stirring to melt the butter and mix everything together into a smooth, brown sauce.

STIR WELL, and bring the frosting to a lively boil, stirring often. Adjust the heat to maintain an active but gentle boil, and cook for 5 minutes, stirring often. When the frosting begins to thicken, remove it from the heat, stir in the vanilla, and set it aside to cool for about 20 minutes.

BEAT THE FROSTING just until it thickens and looks shiny, and then spread it over the cake or the layers you want to ice.

This icing is the great-grandmother of **Seven-Minute Frosting** (page 147). It predates the mixer, stoves powered by gas or electricity, the candy thermometer, and the refrigerator. Boiled icing traditionally provided the crowning finish for such family heirloom recipes as **Lane Cake** (page 38), **Lady Baltimore Cake** (page 40), and **Classic Coconut Cake** (page 58). Having a helper when you make this icing is a grand idea, as boiled icing involves a bit more hands-on work than most modern recipes. Boiled icing is at its best the day it is made.

Boiled Icing

MAKES ENOUGH FOR ONE 3-LAYER CAKE

- 1 cup sugar
- ½ cup water
- 2 egg whites

STIR THE SUGAR into the water to dissolve it. Bring the mixture to a gentle boil, and cook without stirring for 3 minutes. Then boil for 5 to 10 minutes more, stirring often, until the syrup has thickened and will form itself into a thread 2 inches long when poured from a spoon back into the pot. Set the syrup aside.

BEAT THE EGG WHITES in a large bowl with a mixer at high speed until they are bright white, shiny, and pillow into voluminous clouds. While still beating, slowly pour the cooked syrup into the egg whites to blend them together into one fluffy white icing, 4 to 5 minutes.

QUICKLY SPREAD THE ICING on the cake, and let stand at room temperature for 1 hour to set up. Cover the cake carefully and refrigerate briefly. The icing is best if made, used, and enjoyed the same day.

I adore this simple, creamy icing, which I first encountered on a **Red Velvet Cake** (page 103), studded with finely chopped pecans and shredded coconut. Try this icing with applesauce cakes and spice cakes, too, as an alternative to cream cheese frosting. All it requires is a little cooking on top of the stove to mix the flour and milk into a velvety base for the frosting. Then it's as easy as beating butter and sugar together, along with a flavoring, and you have a velvet-smooth, irresistible icing for your favorite cakes. Keep cakes with this icing refrigerated except around serving time, since it is based on butter and milk.

Vanilla Cream Icing

MAKES ENOUGH FOR ONE 3-LAYER CAKE, ONE 13-BY-9-INCH CAKE, OR 24 CUPCAKES

- 1 cup milk
- 2 tablespoons all-purpose flour
- 1 cup (2 sticks) butter, softened
- 1 cup sugar
- 1 teaspoon vanilla extract

COMBINE the milk and flour in a small or medium saucepan. Cook over medium heat for 3 to 5 minutes, stirring often and well with a whisk or large spoon, until the mixture becomes thick, shiny, and white, like very softly whipped cream. Set aside to cool.

TO COMPLETE THE FROSTING, beat the butter with a mixer at high speed until light and fluffy. Add the sugar in 3 batches, beating well each time. Add the vanilla and then the thick, cooled milk mixture. Beat for about 2 minutes more, stopping often to scrape down the bowl, until the icing is fluffy and soft, and thick enough to spread.

This marvelous little recipe makes an outstanding, fudgy icing with very little effort. It sets up smooth and luscious, a neat and inviting finish for any cake. This is one of many excellent recipes Blanche Williams of Durham, North Carolina, contributed to *Watts Cooking Now?*, a fund-raising cookbook compiled by the Watts Street Baptist Church. Have the cake layers handy so that you can spread the icing over them as soon as it is ready.

Blanche's Never-Fail Chocolate Icing

MAKES ENOUGH FOR ONE 2-LAYER CAKE OR ONE 13-BY-9-INCH CAKE

2 cups sugar

2/3 cup evaporated milk

1/2 cup (1 stick) butter

1 cup semisweet chocolate chips or chopped semisweet chocolate

1 teaspoon vanilla extract

IN A MEDIUM SAUCEPAN over low heat, combine the sugar, evaporated milk, and butter. Cook slowly, stirring to dissolve the sugar and melt the butter. Increase the heat just enough to bring the mixture to a boil, and then let it boil for 2 minutes. Remove from the heat, add the chocolate chips, and beat until smooth. Stir in the vanilla. Spread over the cake, or the layers you want to ice.

This gives you the luscious pleasure of caramel icing without the effort and care needed for caramelizing sugar. The texture is perfect for covering a pound cake or Bundt cake, or icing the top of a layer cake so that the extra frosting trickles down the sides. If you want more of a thick, fudgy caramel frosting than a rich glaze, see **Gigi's Fabulous Caramel Cake** (page 52). This caramel glaze sets up quickly and needs to be spread on the cake as soon as it's ready.

Caramel Glaze

MAKES ENOUGH FOR ONE 3-LAYER CAKE, 1 TUBE OR BUNDT CAKE, OR ONE 13-BY-9-INCH CAKE

½ cup (1 stick) butter
1 cup light brown sugar
½ cup evaporated milk
4 cups sifted confectioners' sugar
1 teaspoon vanilla

COMBINE the butter and brown sugar in a medium saucepan. Stir over medium heat until the butter melts and blends with the brown sugar to make a smooth sauce, 2 to 3 minutes. Add the milk, and let the icing come to a gentle boil. Stir well, remove from the heat, and add the sifted confectioners' sugar and the vanilla. Beat well with a mixer, whisk, or spoon for 1 or 2 minutes, until the glaze thickens and loses a little of its shine. Use at once. If the glaze hardens, stir in 1 or 2 spoonfuls of evaporated milk to soften it.

You will find lemon curd listed as "lemon jelly" and "lemon filling" in Southern recipes. Regardless of what it is called, its flavor is exquisite. A few ingredients, a little stove time, and there you stand with an absolute sunburst of ravishing, sweet, and tangy tastes. It looks lovely, keeps beautifully, makes a fine gift, and works right alongside jam, jelly, and honey on the table when it's time for breakfast or a tea party. Use a double boiler if you have one; if not, create one out of a heat-proof bowl and a saucepan. Stainless steel mixing bowls are perfect for this task. Be sure that the bowl fits snugly and securely over the pot of water, and have a pot holder or folded kitchen towel handy for holding onto the hot bowl as the lemon curd cooks.

Lemon Curd

MAKES 1½ CUPS

- 3 eggs
- ¾ cup sugar
- ⅓ cup freshly squeezed lemon juice (use 3 or 4 lemons)
- 1 tablespoon finely grated lemon zest
- 6 tablespoons cold butter

BRING ABOUT 3 INCHES OF WATER to a lively simmer in the bottom of a double boiler or medium saucepan. Meanwhile, combine the eggs, sugar, lemon juice, and lemon zest in the top of the double boiler or a heat-proof bowl that will fit snugly over the saucepan. Whisk or stir with a fork to mix them together very well. Cut the butter into small chunks.

COOK THE EGG-AND-LEMON MIXTURE over the simmering water, whisking and stirring often and well, for 8 to 10 minutes, until it thickens to a luxurious, bright yellow sauce with a consistency like lightly whipped cream. Remove from the heat and stir in the butter, a few chunks at a time, whisking to melt the chunks into the lemon curd before adding the next batch.

COOL TO ROOM TEMPERATURE, and then transfer the lemon curd to a glass jar. Store it, covered, in the refrigerator for up to 2 weeks.

This Colonial American version of crème anglaise is still enjoyed in Southern homes, particularly in Kentucky and the deep South, and especially during the Christmas holiday season. Use it in **Alice Lenora Duke Wooten's Tipsey Cake** (page 88), or as an accompaniment to one of the rich layer cakes in the "Chocolate Cakes, Southern Style" section (pages 130–143).

Boiled Custard

MAKES ABOUT 2 CUPS

- 2 cups milk
- 5 tablespoons all-purpose flour
- ¾ cup sugar
- ⅛ teaspoon salt
- 4 egg yolks, beaten
- 1 teaspoon vanilla extract

HEAT THE MILK in a medium saucepan over medium-high heat until it is very hot and steaming, but not quite boiling. Bring about 3 inches of water to a lively simmer in the bottom of a double boiler or a medium saucepan.

MEANWHILE, in the top of the double boiler or a heat-proof bowl that will fit snugly over the saucepan, combine the flour, sugar, and salt and stir to mix them well. Place the top of the double boiler or the bowl over the simmering water. Slowly stir in the scalded milk, and cook, stirring often, until the mixture thickens, 5 to 10 minutes.

COMBINE THE EGG YOLKS in a medium bowl, and then slowly whisk in about half of the hot milk mixture to warm the eggs. Pour the warmed egg yolks into the hot milk and cook for 2 to 5 minutes more, stirring often. Add the vanilla, stir to mix well, and remove from the heat. Cool the custard to room temperature, and then press a sheet of plastic wrap directly onto the surface of the custard and refrigerate. It will keep for up to 3 days.

BIBLIOGRAPHY

Anderson, Jean. *The American Century Cookbook.* New York: Clarkson Potter, 1997.

Auchmutey, Jim, and Mara Reid Rogers. *The South the Beautiful Cookbook: Authentic Recipes from the American South.* San Francisco: Collins, 1996.

Bailey, Cornelia Walker, Yvonne J. Grovner, and William "Doc Bill" Thomas. *The Foods of Georgia's Barrier Islands: A Gourmet Food Guide to Native American, Geechee and European Influences on the Golden Isles.* Gainesville, GA: Georgia Design and Graphics, 2000.

Bailey, Cornelia Walker. *God, Dr. Buzzard, and the Bolito Man.* New York: Random House, 2000.

Bailey, Phoebe. *An African American Cookbook: Traditional and Other Favorite Recipes.* Intercourse, PA: Good Books, 2002.

Beranbaum, Rose Levy. *The Cake Bible.* New York, William Morrow, 1988.

Brown, Marion. *Marion Brown's Southern Cookbook.* Chapel Hill: The University of North Carolina Press, 1951. Reprinted by Gramercy Books, 2001.

Buttross, Waddad Habeeb. *Waddad's Kitchen: Lebanese Zest and Southern Best.* Natchez, MS: Waddad Habeeb Buttross, 1982.

Claiborne, Craig. *Craig Claiborne's Southern Cooking.* New York: Times Books/Random House, 1987.

Collin, Rima and Richard. *The New Orleans Cookbook: Creole, Cajun, and Louisiana French Recipes Past and Present.* New York: Alfred A. Knopf, 1996.

Corriher, Shirley. *Cookwise: Secrets of Cooking Revealed.* New York: Random House, 1998.

Council, Mildred. *Mama Dip's Family Cookbook.* Chapel Hill: The University of North Carolina Press, 2005.

———. *Mama Dip's Kitchen.* Chapel Hill: The University of North Carolina Press, 1999.

Dabney, Joseph E. *Smokehouse Ham, Spoon Bread & Scuppernong Wine: The Folklore and Art of Southern Appalachian Cooking.* Nashville: Cumberland House, 1998.

Darden, Norma Jean, and Carole Darden. *Spoonbread and Strawberry Wine: Recipes and Remembrances of a Family.* New York: Anchor Press, 1978.

Dixon, Ethel, Charlene Johnson, and Wayne Tanner. *Big Mama's Old Black Pot Recipes.* Alexandria, LA: Stoke Gabriel, 1987.

Dull, Henrietta Stanley. *Southern Cooking.* Atlanta: Ruralist Press, 1928. Reprinted by Cherokee Press, 1989.

Dupree, Nathalie. *New Southern Cooking with Nathalie Dupree.* New York: Alfred A. Knopf, 1993.

———. *Nathalie Dupree's Southern Memories: Recipes and Reminiscences.* New York: Clarkson Potter, 1993.

Eakin, Katherine M., and Annette Thompson, editors. *The Southern Heritage Cakes Cookbook.* Birmingham, AL: Oxmoor House, 1983

Edge, John T. *A Gracious Plenty: Recipes and Recollections from the American South.* New York: G.P. Putnam's Sons, 1999.

Egerton, John. *Side Orders: Small Helpings of Southern Cookery and Culture.* Atlanta: Peachtree Publishers, 1990.

Egerton, John, and Ann Bleidt Egerton. *Southern Food: At Home, on the Road, in History.* Chapel Hill: The University of North Carolina Press, 1993.

Estes, Rufus. *Rufus Estes' Good Things to Eat: The First Cookbooks by an African-American Chef.* Mineola, NY: Dover Publications, 2004. Originally published as *Good Things to Eat, As Suggested by Rufus.* Chicago: Rufus B. Estes, 1911.

Evert, Jodi, editor. *Felicity's 1774 Cookbook: A Peek at Dining in the Past with Meals You Can Make Today.* Middleton, WI: Pleasant Company, 1994.

Ferguson, Sheila. *Soul Food: Classic Cuisine from the Deep South.* New York: Weidenfeld and Nicholson, 1989.

Ferris, Marcie Cohen. *Matzoh Ball Gumbo: Culinary Tales of the Jewish South.* Chapel Hill: The University of North Carolina Press, 2005.

Fisher, Abby. *What Mrs. Fisher Knows About Old Southern Cooking: Soups, Pickles, Preserves, Etc.* San Francisco Women's Cooperative Printing Office, 1881. Facsimile edition. Reprinted by Applewood Books, 1995.

Flagg, Fannie. *Fannie Flagg's Original Whistle Stop Cafe Cookbook.* New York: Ballantine, 1993.

Fowler, Damon Lee. *Classical Southern Cooking: A Celebration of the Cuisine of the Old South.* New York: Crown, 1995.

Glenn, Camille. *The Heritage of Southern Cooking.* New York: Workman, 1986.

Grosvenor, Verta Mae. *Vibration Cooking: The Travel Notes of a Geechee Girl.* New York: Doubleday, 1970.

Harris, Jessica B. *Beyond Gumbo: Creole Fusion Food from the Atlantic Rim.* New York: Simon and Schuster, 2003.

——. *The Welcome Table: African-American Heritage Cooking.* New York: Simon and Schuster, 1995.

Hess, Karen. *The Carolina Rice Kitchen: The African Connection.* University of South Carolina Press, 1992.

Hodgson, Moira. *Fruitcake Favorites: Recipes, Legends, and Lore from the World's Best Cooks and Eaters.* San Francisco: HarperCollins, 1993.

Joachim, David. *The Food Substitutions Bible.* Toronto: Robert Rose, 2005.

Jones, Wilbert. *Mama's Tea Cakes: 101 Delicious Soul Food Desserts.* New York: Birch Lane Press/Kensington, 1998.

Kleinman, Kathryn. *Birthday Cakes: Recipes and Memories from Celebrated Bakers.* San Francisco: Chronicle Books, 2004.

Lewis, Edna. *In Pursuit of Flavor.* New York: Alfred A. Knopf, 1988.

——. *The Taste of Country Cooking.* New York: Alfred A. Knopf, 1976.

Lundy, Ronni. *Butter Beans to Blackberries: Recipes from the Southern Garden.* New York: North Point Press/Farrar, Straus and Giroux, 1999.

McFeely, William S. *Sapelo's People: A Long Walk into Freedom.* New York: W. W. Norton, 1994.

McGee, Harold. *On Food and Cooking: The Science and Lore of the Kitchen.* New York: Scribner's, 2004.

McNair, James. *James McNair's Cakes.* San Francisco: Chronicle Books, 1994.

Metcalfe, Gayden, and Charlotte Hayes. *Being Dead Is No Excuse: The Official Southern Ladies Guide to Hosting the Perfect Funeral.* New York: Hyperion, 2005.

Neal, Bill. *Bill Neal's Southern Cooking.* Chapel Hill: The University of North Carolina Press, 1985.

——. *Biscuits, Spoonbread, and Sweet Potato Pie.* Chapel Hill: The University of North Carolina Press, 1991.

Page, Linda Garland, and Eliot Wigginton, editors. *The Foxfire Book of Appalachian Cookery.* Chapel Hill: The University of North Carolina Press, 1992.

Parker, Curtis. *The Lost Art of Scratch Cooking: Recipes from the Kitchen of Natha Adkins Parker.* Elk Grove, CA: Curtis Parker, 1997.

Peacock, Scott, and Edna Lewis. *The Gift of Southern Cooking.* New York: Alfred A. Knopf, 2002.

Pressly, Sybil. *The Mast Farm Inn: Family Style.* Valle Crucis, NC: Sybil Pressly, 1993.

Prudhomme, Paul. *Chef Paul Prudhomme's Louisiana Kitchen.* New York: William Morrow, 1984.

——. *The Prudhomme Family Cookbook: Old-Time Louisiana Recipes by the Eleven Prudhomme Brothers and Sisters and Chef Paul Prudhomme.* New York: William Morrow, 1987.

Robinson, Sallie Anne. *Gullah Home Cooking the Daufuskie Way: Smokin' Joe Butter Beans, Ol' 'Fuskie Fried Crab Rice, Sticky Bush Blackberry Dumpling, and other Sea Island Favorites.* Chapel Hill, NC: The University of North Carolina Press, 2003.

Rogers, Amy. *Hungry for Home: Stories of Food from Across the Carolinas.* Charlotte: Novello Festival Press, 2003.

Rudisill, Marie. *Fruitcake: Memories of Truman Capote and Sook.* Athens, GA: Hill Street Press, 2000.

Sanders, Dori. *Dori Sanders' Country Cooking: Recipes and Stories from the Family Farm Stand.* Chapel Hill, NC: Algonquin, 1995.

Sax, Richard. *Classic Home Desserts: A Treasury of Heirloom and Contemporary Desserts from Around the World.* Boston: Chapters/Houghton Mifflin, 1994.

Starr, Kathy. *The Soul of Southern Cooking.* Jackson: University Press of Mississippi, 1989.

Tartan, Beth. *North Carolina and Old Salem Cookery.* Chapel Hill, NC: The University of North Carolina Press, 1955. Reprinted in 1992.

Taylor, John Martin. *Hoppin' John's Low Country Cooking.* New York: Bantam Books, 1992.

Thibodaux Service League. *Louisiana Legacy: A Rich Tradition of Artistry with Food and Joy in Life.* Thibodaux, LA: Thibodaux Service League, 1982.

Thurman, Sue Bailey, editor. *The Historical Cookbook of the American Negro.* The National Council of Negro Women: 1958. Facsimile edition. Reprinted by Beacon Press, 2000.

Tillery, Carolyn Quick. *The African-American Heritage Cookbook: Traditional Recipes and Fond Remembrances from Alabama's Renowned Tuskegee Institute.* New York: Citadel Press/Kensington, 1996.

——. *A Taste of Freedom: A Cookbook with Recipes and Remembrances from the Hampton Institute.* New York: Citadel Press/Kensington, 2002.

Watts Street Baptist Church. *Watts Cooking Now?* Durham, NC: Watts Street Baptist Church, 2000.

White, Joyce. *Brown Sugar: Soul Food Desserts from Family and Friends.* New York: HarperCollins, 2003.

Whiting, Helen Hudson. *In Helen's Kitchen: A Philosophy of Food.* Durham, NC: The Regulator Bookshop, 2000.

Wilson, Charles R., and William Ferris, editors. *The Encyclopedia of Southern Culture.* Oxford, MS: Center for the Study of Southern Culture, 1989.

Zanger, Mark H. *The American History Cookbook.* Westport, CT: Greenwood Press, 2003.

MAIL-ORDER AND INTERNET SOURCES

for equipment and ingredients

THE BAKER'S CATALOGUE AT KING ARTHUR FLOUR
58 Billings Farm Road
White River Junction, VT 05051
(800) 827-6836
www.bakerscatalogue.com
Nested sets of stainless steel mixing bowls, dried and candied fruit, rosewater, almond paste, and gel paste food coloring.

CHOCOLATESOURCE.COM
9 Crest Road
Wellesley, MA 02482
(800) 214-4926
www.chocolatesource.com
Valrhona, Callebaut, and other chocolates for baking; cocoa and white chocolate.

GEECHEE SWEETS
P.O. Box 34
Sapelo Island, GA 31327
(912) 485-2262 or (912) 485-2206
www.geecheesweets.com
Jams, jellies, preserves, handcrafts, and books by Mrs. Cornelia Walker Bailey.

HAMMON'S PANTRY
P.O. Box 140
Stockton, MO 65785
(800) 872-6879
www.hammonspantry.com
Black walnuts, whole and chopped, for baking; in-shell black walnuts and special nutcracker designed for this exceptionally hard-shelled nut.

HOPPIN' JOHN'S
(800) 828-4412
www.hoppinjohns.com
Excellent Southern cookbooks by John Martin Taylor, authority on Low Country culinary traditions and history; artisan food items from the South.

KALUSTYANS
123 Lexington Avenue
New York, NY 10016
(212) 685-3451 or (800) 352-3451
www.kalustyans.com
Rosewater and orange flower water, spices, dried unsweetened coconut, almonds, almond paste, pistachios, and peanuts.

PASTRY CHEF CENTRAL
1355 West Palmetto Park Road, Suite 302
Boca Raton, FL 33486
(888) 750-2433
www.pastrychef.com
Kitchen parchment, chocolate, almond paste, cake pans, and various tools for baking.

PENZEYS SPICES
P.O. Box 924
Brookfield, WI 53008
(800) 741-7787
www.penzeys.com
The finest spices, cocoa, extracts, and flavorings, presented in a handsome catalogue filled with recipes, stories, and background information on spices from around the world.

THE SOUTHERN FOODWAYS ALLIANCE
CENTER FOR THE STUDY OF SOUTHERN CULTURE
Barnard Observatory
University, MS 38677
(662) 915-5993
sfamail.olemiss.edu
www.southernfoodways.com
An organization dedicated to finding, celebrating, and preserving Southern culinary traditions and the people and stories behind them.

STEEN'S PURE CANE SYRUP
The C.S. Steen Syrup Mill, Inc.
119 North Main Street
P.O. Box 339
Abbeville, LA 70510
(800) 725-1654
www.steensyrup.com
Louisiana's original pure cane syrup.

SUNNYLAND FARMS PECANS
P.O. Box 8200
Albany, GA 42706
(800) 999-2488
www.sunnylandfarms.com
Whole and chopped pecans, walnuts, almonds, dates, figs, and glacé apricots.

SUR LA TABLE
P.O. Box 34707
Seattle, WA 98124
(800) 243-0852
www.surlatable.com
Double boilers, wire cooling racks, cake pans, thermometers, measuring cups and spoons, sifters, cake stands, and various other tools.

SWEET CELEBRATIONS
(formerly Maid of Scandinavia)
P.O. Box 39426
Edina, MN 55439
(800) 328-6722
www.sweetc.com
White chocolate, almond paste, cake pans, gel paste food coloring, flavorings, and cake-decorating supplies.

WHITE LILY FLOUR COMPANY
P.O. Box 871
Knoxville, TN 37901
(800) 264-5459
www.whitelily.com
Soft wheat-flour, which is traditional in Southern baking, particularly for cakes and biscuits.

WILLIAMS-SONOMA
P.O. Box 7456
San Francisco, CA 94120
(800) 541-2233
www.williams-sonoma.com
Cake pans, spatulas, mixing bowls, measuring cups and spoons, extracts, timers, and cake stands in various sizes.

PERMISSIONS

WADDAD HABEEB BUTTROSS'S CLASSIC POUND CAKE (page 20) from *Waddad's Kitchen: Lebanese Zest and Southern Best*, by Waddad Habeeb Buttross (Natchez, MS: self-published, 1982).

MISS EDNA FAUST'S BLUE RIBBON POUND CAKE (page 27) contributed by Edna Faust of Durham, NC, to *Hungry for Home: Stories of Food from Across the Carolinas* (Charlotte: Novello Festival Press, 2003) and *Red Pepper Fudge and Blue Ribbon Biscuits: Favorite Stories and Recipes from North Carolina State Fair Winners* (Winston-Salem, NC: Down Home Press/John F. Blair, 1995), both by Amy Rogers.

GEORGE PYNE'S BOURBON POUND CAKE (page 28) by George Pyne, with the kind permission of the Pyne family, Durham, NC.

COLONIAL QUEEN CAKES (page 34) from *Felicity's Cookbook: A Peek at Dining in the Past with Meals You Can Cook Today*, by Polly Athan, Rebecca Sample Bernstein, Terri Braun, and Jodi Evert (Middleton, WI: Pleasant Company Publications, 1994).

KATHY STARR'S MISSISSIPPI DELTA JELLY CAKE (page 37) from *The Soul of Southern Cooking* by Kathy Starr (Jackson, MS: The University Press, 1989; reissued by NewSouth Books, Montgomery, AL, 2002).

DR. GEORGE WASHINGTON CARVER'S METROPOLITAN CAKE WITH PEANUTS (page 44) from "How to Grow the Peanut and 105 Ways of Preparing It for Human Consumption," *Bulletin #31*, June, 1925, by Dr. George Washington Carver (Tuskegee, AL: Tuskegee Institute National Historic Site, Dr. George Washington Carver National Monument, reprinted 1983).

MASHULA'S COCONUT CAKE (page 70) created by Ann Romines, Director of the Graduate Program and Professor of English at The George Washington University, published in *Eudora Welty Newsletter XXVIII*, Winter 2004.

EUDORA WELTY'S WHITE FRUITCAKE (page 76) from Miss Eudora Welty's holiday greeting card of 1980, with the kind permission of Eudora Welty, LLC, Jackson, MS.

ALICE LENORA DUKE WOOTEN'S TIPSEY CAKE (page 88) contributed by Marilyn Meacham Price of Fort Mill, SC, to *Hungry for Home: Stories of Food from Across the Carolinas* by Amy Rogers.

SISTER SADIE'S ROSH HASHANAH HONEY CAKE (page 91) from *Matzoh Ball Gumbo: Culinary Tales of the Jewish South* by Marcie Cohen Ferris (Chapel Hill, NC: The University of North Carolina Press, 2005).

THIBODAUX CHOCOLATE DOBERGE CAKE (page 107) from *Louisiana Legacy: A Rich Tradition of Artistry with Food and Joy in Life*, by the Thibodaux Service League (Thibodaux, LA: self-published, 1982).

CORNELIA WALKER BAILEY'S PEAR BREAD (page 114) and SAPELO ISLAND HARD TIME CAKE (page 119) by Cornelia Walker Bailey, from *The Foods of Georgia's Barrier Islands: A Gourmet Food Guide to Native American, Geechee and European Influences on the Golden Isles* by Yvonne Y. Grovner, Cornelia Walker Bailey, and William Doc Bill Thomas (Gainesville, GA: Georgia Design and Graphics, 2000).

SALLIE ANNE ROBINSON'S DAUFUSKIE ISLAND CARROT CAKE (page 118) from *Gullah Home Cooking the Daufuskie Way: Smokin' Joe Butter Beans, Ol' 'Fuskie Fried Crab Rice, Sticky-Bush Blackberry Dumpling, and Other Sea Island Favorites* by Sallie Anne Robinson (Chapel Hill, NC: The University of North Carolina Press, 2003).

SHENANDOAH VALLEY BLUEBERRY CAKE (page 124) from *Best of the Bushel*, published by the Junior League of Charlottesville, VA, 1984.

SYBIL PRESSLY'S BUTTERMILK CAKE WITH OLD-FASHIONED CHOCOLATE ICING (page 132) from *Mast Farm Inn: Family Style* by Sybil Pressly (Valle Crucis, NC: self-published, 1993).

HELEN HUDSON WHITING'S CELESTIAL CHOCOLATE CAKE (page 138) from *In Helen's Kitchen: A Philosophy of Food*, by Helen Hudson Whiting (Durham, NC: The Regulator Bookshop, 2000).

BLANCHE'S NEVER-FAIL CHOCOLATE ICING (page 154) contributed by Blanche Williams of Durham, NC, to *Watts Cooking Now?*, by the Watts Street Baptist Church (Durham, NC: self-published, 2002).

INDEX

D

E

F

G

H

I

Q

R

S

T

V

W

Y

Table of EQUIVALENTS

THE EXACT EQUIVALENTS IN THE FOLLOWING TABLES HAVE BEEN ROUNDED FOR CONVENIENCE.

LIQUID / DRY MEASURES

U.S.	Metric
1/4 teaspoon	1.25 milliliters
1/2 teaspoon	2.5 milliliters
1 teaspoon	5 milliliters
1 tablespoon (3 teaspoons)	15 milliliters
1 fluid ounce (2 tablespoons)	30 milliliters
1/4 cup	60 milliliters
1/3 cup	80 milliliters
1/2 cup	120 milliliters
1 cup	240 milliliters
1 pint (2 cups)	480 milliliters
1 quart (4 cups, 32 ounces)	960 milliliters
1 gallon (4 quarts)	3.84 liters
1 ounce (by weight)	28 grams
1 pound	448 grams
2.2 pounds	1 kilogram

LENGTHS

U.S.	Metric
1/8 inch	3 millimeters
1/4 inch	6 millimeters
1/2 inch	12 millimeters
1 inch	2.5 centimeters

OVEN TEMPERATURES

Fahrenheit	Celsius	Gas
250	120	1/2
275	140	1
300	150	2
325	160	3
350	180	4
375	190	5
400	200	6
425	220	7
450	230	8
475	240	9
500	260	10